IRELAND FROM THE AIR

IRELAND

from the Air

Daphne D. C. Pochin Mould

David & Charles : Newton Abbot

0 7153 5758 1

© DAPHNE D. C. POCHIN MOULD 1972

Set in 11 on 12 Modern
by C. E. Dawkins (Typesetters) Limited London SE1
and printed in Great Britain
by Latimer Press Limited Whitstable
for David & Charles (Publishers) Limited
South Devon House Newton Abbot Devon

CONTENTS

1 DISCOVERING IRELAND FROM THE AIR

Long ago, when flight was only just being attempted, G. K. Chesterton wrote in 'The Club of Queer Trades' that 'to talk on the top of a hill is superb, but to talk on the top of a flying hill is a fairy tale'. His flying hill was merely a London tramcar, but the light plane really does give the flying hill view of the world, making its own mountain peak wherever its pilot chooses. Nearly all the pictures in this book might have been taken from the top of a mountain, more especially a fairly precipitous mountain if there had happened to be one in the vicinity. In technical terms they are 'obliques', not the direct down, map-maker's 'verticals' taken to give a plan of the world below. Vertical air photos are much harder to 'read' for the ordinary person; obliques, taken out of the aeroplane's windows, make their points immediately.

There are few countries with more possibilities for the air photographer than Ireland, few countries whose colour and beauty is brighter, or at times almost overwhelming in its sheer splendour. Set on the western seaboard of Europe, this small offshore island is a place of mild moist winds, of a climate that varies not only from day to day, but from place to place on the same day. When it is fine, the visibility can be very great, so that it is possible to see over almost the whole length of the country. It is green most of the year round, but the grass, kept so green by the rain, is set off by a brilliance of other colours through the year. There is the golden riot of furze (gorse/whin) blossom edging the roads and spreading over hillside and waste ground, to be followed by the white of blackthorn and later hawthorn blossom in the hedges; then come rhododendrons turning hillsides a delicate purple, and later the heather, and the bronze and gold and yellow of autumn; in winter, there is the snow on the high peaks.

Ireland is a small country, but one of enormous variety, each of its miniature mountain lines different from every other. Its rivers follow peculiar courses over the inland plains; its cliffs, high and magnificent, rim long strands on which the waves, seen from above, break like white lace. It is a country rich in the history which seems in some districts to be marked on every field in traces of old earthworks, and where the changing light and changing vegetation can make every flight a voyage of discovery of new remains or new information about old ones.

To come into Ireland from Britain is to see a long coastline ahead, with mountains rising from it here and there. Come down the Firth of Clyde, past the great rock of Ailsa Craig, and ahead is the low dark line of the Irish coast at Island Magee. To head inland, to land at Belfast's airfield (Aldergrove) is to meet the first of Ireland's several vast inland 'seas', the great freshwater lake of Lough Neagh, but to head south takes one down the long sea inlet that the Vikings called Strangford (fiord). Below are the great round walls of Nendrum, an early Celtic monastery, and beyond, the lumpy ridge of the Mountains of Mourne. Of granite, with tors on some of their ridges, the Silent Valley reservoir winding into their heart, they are, from the air, far less striking than the other

1 Drogheda on the river Boyne, whose mouth, on the Irish Channel, can be seen in the distance. The original town was on the river bank at the bridge, and its outlines are marked by the cluster of church spires. The modern city has spread widely into suburbia and new development. The Dublin-Belfast railway crosses the river below the road bridge. The smoking chimney belongs to a large cement factory. The name is Droichead Atha, 'Bridge of the Ford' but the place is identified with ancient Inver Colpa.

Irish hills. Across Carlingford (fiord) Lough, another sea inlet, is Carlingford mountain, all rough gabbro outcropping through the heather, and south, toward Dublin, a low coast and a vast plain reaching into the Irish heartland and beyond. Here, around Mourne and Cavan, the land is ice-moulded into innumerable little ridges, *drumlins* as the Irish name calls them, but south, into Meath are the great farmlands that are the richest in all Ireland, with the low rise of the hill of

Tara set among them. So low is the hill of Tara that only from the air can you really see it at all, and on a hazy day the plains around fade into blue distance.

Here too is the mouth of the Boyne and above it the old town of Drogheda, and above that, on the river bank, the great Megalithic tombs of Dowth, Newgrange and Knowth, with many more less obvious remains on the ground around them. Then Dublin Bay, and the city sprawling in suburban jungles over either side of the arc of the bay. A place to come to by night when the city is a sparkling sea of stars and the water's edge is rimmed by the street lights. On a clear day you can see from the Mourne and Carlingford mountains to the north down to the Wicklow ones to the south.

The Wicklow mountains are granite like the Mournes, but of another geological age and quite different in character. They are mountains of high, broad heathery backs,

8

with deep cut corries and glens, like the valley of Glendalough with the round tower of St Kevin's monastery. Between mountain and east coast is a green fertile plain and deep dry valleys cut by water from the melting ice sheets of the Ice Age. The hillsides have some scraps of native oakwood, and the pilot sees them in the first golden leaf of spring or russet in autumn, before going southward to Wexford at the southeastern corner of the island. This is an area isolated from the rest of Ireland by river and hill, green and fertile, with lakes held back

2 Fields with ring forts in low evening October sunshine in county Sligo. This is typical of the way the old 'forts' (farmsteads) occur in good farmland, dotted here and there just like the modern farm houses.

by sand bars along its southern coast. At Wexford harbour, on the reclaimed slobs, vast numbers of geese winter in the bird sanctuaries there, and yet other migrant birds make landfall on the Saltee islands off the Wexford coast.

Westward at Waterford is a complex sea

3 A detail of the sea cliffs of Slieve League, county Donegal.

4 A close up of the new Irish cottages for visitors in Glencolumbcille.

inlet—Wexford and Waterford were both places settled by the Vikings who began town life in Ireland—and into this shining expanse of water come the Three Sisters, the great rivers of Barrow, Nore and Suir. They rise near each other but follow different paths to the sea.

There are more mountains, the corrie-etched crags of the Comeraghs; more cliffs and strands between, and then the complex inlet of Cork Harbour with the river Lee flowing into it, and Cork, the second city of the Irish Republic, spreading out from its valley nucleus to the surrounding ridges.

5 Glendalough, the glen of the two lakes, in the Wicklow mountains. This is probably the most famous glen in Ireland, famous both for its beauty and for the important monastic remains of the six-century foundation of St Kevin. It was an important ecclesiastical centre for many centuries. Kevin came first to settle as a hermit on the cragside up valley; disciples joined him and the monastery was established between the two lakes. Later it extended still more to a point below the second lake where are now a round tower and ancient churches. This is a typical Wicklow glen, straight, over-deepened by ice and with craggy flanks.

Westward from Cork the land visibly roughens, rich fields giving place to tiny,

6 The Barrow (left) joins with the Nore (right). In the distance is Waterford Harbour and, to the left, the smoke hangs over New Ross. (For other river Nore subjects, see plates 27, 36.)

stone-walled ones through whose thin skin of soil the rock breaks. Here in the south-west, in Cork and Kerry, Irish scenery reaches a peak of colour, variety and form. Here are the wild high ridges of the country's highest mountains, and a wonderland of lakes, upon the lowland and in steps up the hillsides, corrie set above corrie, with tarns in the moorland of the summit plateaux. Here the islands begin; Carbery's Hundred Isles in west Cork, and the rocky fangs of the Bull, Scellig, Tearaght; the storied Blaskets which lead to the long series of islands up the west coast.

Northward is the Mouth of the Shannon, the greatest river in all Britain and Ireland, a watery highway through the length of Ireland, edged with historic remains for all its 200 miles. On the estuary shore is the international airport of Shannon, and the older, now deserted, transatlantic flying-boat base of Foynes. On the north bank of the Shannon is county Clare which leads into a world of grey terraced hills of bare limestone to whose shoulders cling thicket woods and whose surfaces are a mosaic of old fields, old churches and old forts.

Out to sea, the limestone 'karst' is continued in the three grey rocks of the Aran islands with their huge stone forts set in a maze of stone-walled fields, whilst on Inishmore, sheer cliffs fall 200 or 300ft to the Atlantic.

At the head of Galway Bay you can look east over the vast inland plain that stretches all the way to the east coast at Dublin. To the west and north are the shining inland 'seas' of Loughs Corrib and Mask, the quartzite mountains of the Twelve Bens and Maumturks rising from the low lake-studded moorland of coastal Connemara. Northward yet is the long arm of Killary, the only real fiord in Ireland, and Clare Island out to sea;

Croagh Patrick is close at hand with the white pilgrim path climbing to its summit chapel. The drumlin swarms come down to the sea at Westport at the head of Clew Bay, and end in a maze of tiny islets, each formed by a ridge crest. Ahead to the north, are the very different rounded heights of the Nephin

7 The Great Scellig, Scellig of St Michael, patron of high places. There are the remains of a sixth-century monastery built in drystone, with beehive huts and oratories on the shoulder nearest the camera. The lighthouse is at the other end facing the open sea. A helicopter pad has lately been constructed on the rock for the benefit of lighthouse relief.

mountains, and the long low brown moorlands of the Ox mountains. Here the lowland is all speckled with antiquities, with Megalithic cairns and hut circles, and there are here, too, quite different limestone mountains, the green, flat topped heights that end in the snout of Ben Bulbin at Sligo.

The circuit of Ireland is almost completed here, over the strands of Bundoran, the hydro-electricity dam on the river Erne, and the blue eye of the penitential pilgrimage lake of Lough Derg set in brown moors. For this is the north-west, Donegal, with bare low rocky land coming down to an often angry sea. This hard terrain of moor and tiny farm is broken up by great mountains and mountain lines. Slieve League falls to the sea in wild precipices; Errigal's quartzite cone is probably the most dramatic peak in Ireland. The sea winds deep into Ireland here from the north, in the inlets called Lough Foyle and Lough Swilly, hazy blue fingers between

8 Charles Fort, Kinsale, county Cork. For many centuries, Kinsale was an important port and the harbour guarded by Ringcurran fort. The old stronghold was enlarged by the Earl of Orrery, Lord President of Munster, in 1667, and ten years later the construction of the present stone fort began, by the order of the Duke of Ormond. The new structure was named Charles Fort in honour of King Charles II. It has five bastions and once mounted 100 brass cannons.

the hills on either hand, and with Derry on the shores of the head of Lough Swilly. Across the broad ridge of the Sperrin mountains lies Lough Neagh. Out to sea, off the coast of Donegal are yet more islands; the great hump of Aran (to be distinguished from the 'south' Aran islands in Galway Bay) dotted with white houses; and well out to sea, yet looking so close in fine weather, little Tory, with its great cliffs standing out boldly against the blue of the ocean.

It is the purpose of this book to give some idea of this infinitely varied Irish world as it is seen from a light aeroplane flying, in part, the course described above, in part many other courses.

The pictures were all taken by the author,

9 The highest mountains in Ireland, pictured in winter. The MacGillycuddy Reeks in county Kerry terminate in Carrauntual (left centre), at 3,414ft the highest; Beenkeragh (right centre) rises to 3,314ft and Caher (beyond Carrauntual) to 3,200ft. The ridge walk of the three peaks is one of the finest in Ireland. The picture shows also the tiny and inaccessible tarn on the cliffs below Carrauntual, called the Devil's Looking Glass.

who was both pilot and photographer, with an ordinary hand held 35mm camera. For such work a high wing aircraft with a window that can be opened in flight is the most useful, and most of the pictures were taken from such machines—Cessna 172, Cessna 150 and Auster.

15

2 DISCOVERING THE PAST

Wherever man has disturbed the soil by building a wall or digging a ditch, the earth never returns to its original uniformity with the surrounding ground. Traces of the disturbance remain, and these traces the air survey can seek out and record, showing archaeologists where to begin new 'digs', or giving them fuller information of the other remains surrounding the obvious big cairn or ring fort.

Crop marks are the best known trace: young corn growing slightly differently on the once disturbed land so that, in spring, the shadows of old forts and walls show clearly from the air in the growing crop. But a low bright sun in winter, late autumn or early spring, can highlight very low, almost obliterated ridges; or they can be picked out by snow or frost that melts differently on the old ridge or ditch traces. A faint ring fort can show as a brown ring in a white hoar-frosted field as you fly over it on a morning of frost, the rime melting off the old ring first.

Over very considerable areas of Ireland, in suitable low lighting, nearly every field seems to have traces of one sort or another as you fly over it. Pointing out the fact that Ireland is a grazing country, one in which heavy tillage has not been carried out over wide areas, E. R. Norman and J. K. S. St Joseph in their book on Irish aerial photography, *The Early Development of Irish Society* (Cambridge 1969), claim that 'Nowhere else in western Europe are the corrugations of the surface representing activities of ancient man so clearly visible over large areas'.

The Megalithic people came to Ireland perhaps 3,000 years before Christ, perhaps earlier, and they built great chambered stone tombs and stone circles. The great tombs along the Boyne valley, Newgrange, Dowth and Knowth, stand out boldly from the air, and round them are many subsidiary earthworks and marks. From the air one gets a much clearer idea of how any particular structure is sited, and its relation to the geography of the whole countryside round about.

There are many ancient Megalithic cairns in county Sligo, and in that area some striking little green tabletop limestone hills. On one, Knocknashee, there are about fifty hut circles as well as ruined cairns. This extraordinary little hill is ideally suited for defence, with a great outlook over the surrounding plain.

The most prominent and frequent earthwork to be found in Ireland is the ring fort. There are probably upwards of 40,000 of them. Some are obvious, some only to be traced in the difference of colour in newly ploughed land or in crop marks. They are known in folklore as 'fairy forts' and in Irish bear various names, *rath, lios, caiseal* —*rath* being often translated 'fort', *lios* 'enclosure', *caiseal* castle or fort. They are, as has been shown by excavation of some of them, large, fortified farmhouses. The owners were the Irish farmers who lived then, as they live now, in houses scattered over good farm land. From the air it is obvious how the ring forts hug good land or are grouped in almost village–like clusters. Some are of earth, but where stone was plentiful they

are of stone. Inside the huts in the latter areas were stone 'beehive' cells, of which the ruins may yet remain; elsewhere were huts of wood and wattle whose plans the archaeologists have traced from post holes. The fort might have a single enclosing bank and ditch or, in the bigger ones, several. In the absence of wells inside, these forts could only have held out against very brief raiding attacks.

Ireland was then a rural country, without towns. The big farmer needed a strong homestead, and he probably corralled his cattle in the spaces between the several ring walls or in other smaller ring forts near by, for wolves as well as thieves might be abroad.

These ring forts were inhabited over an

10 The crowning glory of the surviving stone forts of Ireland is Dun Conor (Conor's fort) on Inishmaan in the Aran islands of county Galway. This enormous oval structure still encloses the ruins of the owners' beehive huts built in stone, and outside is circled by further defensive walls. Inside the main wall are terraces on which defenders or lookouts could stand. Around it are typical Aran island settlement patterns of bare limestone rock outcrops, small stone-walled fields and little clusters of houses. J. M. Synge stayed in the thatched house, three up from the church on the left of the road, and facing the dun, during most of his time on the Aran islands. The ridges are 'lazy beds' growing potatoes in some of the small fields. These ridges, once dug, are most persistent and mark old cultivations everywhere over Ireland.

11 Ballykinvarga cashel in county Clare. The ring forts were of earth in most places but of dry stone masonry where stone was plentiful. This great 'fort' near Kilfenora adds to its defences a kind of tank trap or chevaux de frise of stones set on edge round the walls. Around it, as over all Burren, is a spider's web of ancient fields and smaller ring forts. More modern fields have straight walls as in the left of the photograph.

immense span of time. Some at Cush in county Limerick, carry a carbon 14 dating of 2600BC. Cahermacnaghten in the Burren in county Clare was inhabited by the O'Davorens who ran a law school there at the end of the seventeenth century. Perhaps the majority may belong to the early Christian,

Celtic Church, period. Garranes, in county Cork, was found to be a factory producing metal work of the sort now represented by such objects as the Tara brooch, and is dated c AD500; Ballycatteen, also in county Cork, to c AD600. Some of the old forts had later Norman mottes or castles built upon them. Excavation showed the beginning of the building of such a motte on the old fort of Beal Boru on the Shannon just above Killaloe; in the Aran islands, the O'Briens' fifteenth-century castle stands inside the stone walls of an earlier rath on Inisheer.

Christianity came to this rural, farming land of Ireland in the fifth century, and spread rapidly. In a country without towns

18

it was almost inevitable that the self-supporting monastery would become the natural unit of the new faith. The whole of Ireland is still overspread with the remains of the monasteries of the Celtic Church, dating from the sixth century on. The secular rath, the big farmer's home, was adapted to monastic use; sometimes, as perhaps on the island of Inismurray, a rath might be given to the church. The monks' cells, a group of small chapels, free standing crosses and, in later centuries, a slender round tower, were grouped within the enclosing walls of earth or stone. Sometimes a church and graveyard are all that remain of such sites, though from the air traces of the great monastic enclosing wall can still be seen surrounding them. But in many cases there are very extensive remains and, again from the air, a fuller and more coherent view of them is obtained. There are the remains of very large monastic establishments such as Clonmacnois, Iniscealtra (both on the Shannon) and Inismurray. There are tiny hermitages scattered amongst the hills, set on lonely islets (Scellig, off the Kerry coast, is the most

12 Mooghaun hilltop fort near Shannon airport in county Clare, the greatest of all Irish hilltop forts. This has walls of stone, and there are three of them, one within the other. The outermost measures 1,500 by 1,000ft. The 'Great Clare Find' of Late Bronze Age gold objects was discovered nearby in 1854, and is possibly associated with this great citadel fortress. Later inhabitants built the small ring forts in and on the older walls with stones from them.

13 The half-circle ring fort: Cahercommaun in county Clare where the enclosing walls back on to an inland cliff in typical Burren country of scrub wood and limestone outcrop. Fully excavated, Cahercommaun was found to have been the castle home of large cattle-raising farmers. It is dated to the early ninth century. Up to forty or fifty people could have lived in Cahercommaun, which they seldom cleaned up; 9,223lb of animal bones were collected from it—97 per cent ox, but including some of the white tailed eagle (extinct in Ireland from the mid-nineteenth century).

dramatic), or on mountain summits. There are islands once on the main sea roads; though now hard to reach by boat, they are easy to see from the air: the Magharees, the Blaskets, the islets off the Mullet peninsula, all with early monastic remains. The large island of Scattery in the Mouth of the Shannon is mostly taken up with a great complex of monastic remains, ranging from early times to medieval rebuildings. There are lake island sites: Church Island in Kerry, Inisfallen at Killarney, to name two. Brendan the Voyager is said to have built the hermitage on the second highest mountain in Ireland, Mount Brandon (3,127ft), where still stand the ruins of beehive cells, beehive oratory, a well, and a surrounding wall. Outside of this, seen from the air, are

14 The adaptation of the ring fort of civilian life to that of the church. Monastic 'cashel' on the island of Illauntannig in the Magharee islands, county Kerry.

St Senach, founder of this monastery, is one of many early Irish saints of whom nothing is known. The shape of the 'cashel' or monastic citadel is typical. There is an outer enclosing ring fort wall. Inside, as in ordinary ring forts, are huts—here beehive drystone ones where the monks lived. There are two rectangular, beehive-roofed oratories or chapels; one, at the new wall, constructed to halt erosion by the sea, is already largely destroyed. The preservation works also included 'tidying up' heaps of stones into the neat piles now seen. Against one is the stone 'high cross' of the monastery; the other is surrounded by a low enclosure. This might be the wall of a round hut from which the tidied up stones fell, or a wall

the fainter traces of two outer walls of the same plan as those of the great stone fort of Dun Aengus in Inishmore, Aran, and Cahercommaun in county Clare.

Cahercommaun has been excavated, and the date is c AD800. Dun Aengus is of unknown date, but with the nearby example of Cahercommaun, is perhaps much later than the pre-historic age often claimed for it. Both these two great 'forts', like the Mount

enclosing another church—or the saint's shrine. Separate walls enclose the several churches of Iniscealtra on the Shannon (see plate 86). It is believed that this photograph is the first to show this low bank round the heap of stones. Discovery of such faint traces is very much a matter of good luck with the sunshine.

15 Dubh Cathair (The Black Fort) on Inishmore in the Aran islands. One of the many headland forts and one of the finest. The massive wall across the headland neck has outworks of up-ended stones forming a chevaux de frise. *There are still the remains of some beehive cells inside the wall; over 100 years ago there were the ruins of more huts on the peninsula snout which can still be seen vaguely from the air in the jumble of stones. Typical of Aran and the Burren are the 'karst' (bare limestone) pavements and sheer cliffs.*

Brandon hermitage, use a natural feature, a cliff, an island precipice, to save building a complete circle of wall.

Both Cahercommaun and Dun Aengus belong to the 'ring fort' type of construction. Another 'fort' style to make good use of a natural feature, is the headland fort. Ireland has a vast number of long, steep-cliffed headlands, and it was very easy to turn them into defensible positions by putting a wall and ditch across the neck. These old defences show up clearly, sometimes dramatically as with the great Black Fort, Dubh Cathair, on Inishmore, Aran. Sometimes the old position might have castles of later date added, the medieval towers on the Old Head of Kinsale in county Cork, for example.

Not all headland forts are on the sea. There is a lake one in Lough Ree on Shannon, where the long snout of the promontory of Rindown is fortified, and on it the ruin of the thirteenth-century castle of the Knights of St John.

Undoubtedly the most dramatic of the 'inland' headland forts is Caherconree, at about 2,000ft on the Slieve Mish mountains in county Kerry. Here a spur on the hillside is defended by a massive stone wall across its neck.

Round these old Celtic sites one can often trace the patterns of their owners' fields. Crop marks around a ring fort may show its fields and out-buildings in plan. Old field walls are very obvious on sites like Iniscealtra or, another early Celtic Church site, round the old churches at Oughtmama in the Burren in county Clare. The old fields are corrugated with the lines of the hand dug 'lazy bed' ridges which are extraordinarily difficult to obliterate completely. In 'lazy bed' cultivation the plot is marked out in narrow strips, manure and/or seaweed is spread on the alternate and undug lengths, and then the soil or sod from the intervening areas is dug out and piled on top of it, producing a broad ridge and furrow pattern. The crop is grown

16 A church site on a lake island: Church Island in Lough Currane near Waterville, county Kerry. The saint of the island is Finan Cam (Squinting Finan) a sixth-century monastic founder. The present remains include a Romanesque church at one end (right in the photo) of the island; old field walls (note hand-dug lazy bed ridges) and farm houses, and a large beehive cell at the other end (left) of the island. Called St Finan's Cell, this structure is believed by Dr Francoise Henry to have been in reality a kiln for drying corn.

This photograph was taken on a day of wind. Note the foam streaks on the water, elongated in the direction in which the wind is blowing, and so crossing the waves at right angles.

17 Hilltop forts were common in early Britain and were occupied when the Romans arrived. They consist of a hilltop fortified by one or more encircling banks following the contour lines. In Ireland they are far less numerous though air survey is helping to discover more of them. Cashel is an impressive example, in county Cork some 10 miles south-west of Cork airport. Typical good Cork farmlands can be seen in the distance.

on the ridges. It is a good way of controlling weeds, and still goes on in fields and gardens in the west of Ireland and Scotland.

In England, hilltop forts, where the actual summit of a hill is defended by concentric banks, are common and were in use when the Romans arrived. In Ireland, they are claimed to be much more rare although in 1971 some fifty-five were known, with others still being discovered. Mooghaun in county Clare, is the most magnificent, with massive stone walls enclosing a rugged little hilltop—walls in which and from which, later round ring forts were built. It lies north of Shannon airport, close to Dromoland Castle.

The majority of hilltop forts are much smaller and less magnificent than Mooghaun.

18 A very large monastic site on Scattery Island in the Shannon estuary. This was founded by St Senan who probably died on 8 March 544. All the buildings are later than his time. Air survey and photography (clearer in colour than in black and white) show the trace of a vast enclosing rath wall, curving round the churches to the left of the round tower, but the whole island would have been monastic property, the monastic buildings enclosed in their rath on it. The round tower, claimed to be the tallest to survive, served as bell tower and refuge. With a single door, the monks and their valuables could be safe here from raiders. The cathedral close to the tower is ninth or tenth century, with an eleventh-century chapel alongside. Senan is buried at Teampall Senan (Senan's church) to the right of the round tower. The holy well is seen as a dark mark just beyond the tower.

One or more defensive banks or walls enclose the hilltop. Sometimes again, the defensive use of the position continued long after the time of the hilltop fort builders. There is, for instance, a medieval castle set within the hilltop fort at Caherdrinny in county Cork near Mitchelstown. From the ground, the broken tooth of the old castle stands out alone; from the air, the line of the hilltop fort walls are clearly seen encircling it, perpetuated in the lines of the present field walls.

Teampall na Marbh (Church of the Dead) at the graveyard by the shore is not earlier than the fourteenth century. Little survives of the castle, to the right of the pier, built c1577.

19 *The half-circle ring fort: Dun Aengus (Angus' Fort) on Inishmore, Aran islands. Here the fort backs on to a sheer limestone cliff, dropping some 200ft to the Atlantic below. The defences include a huge* chevaux de frise *of sharp stones set up on edge. The picture also shows the typical bare limestone 'karst' upland of the Aran islands. Dun Aengus is often claimed to be prehistoric but may in fact be much later, like Cahercommaun that it so closely resembles in plan. Compare Cahercommaun and Dun Aengus with plate 64 of the hermitage on the summit of Mount Brandon.*

20 *Headland fort at 2,000ft on the Slieve Mish mountains in Kerry—Caherconree in winter snow. This site, renowned in Irish folklore, is a massive wall which cuts off the 'headland' spur on the mountain side. (See also plate 56 of these hills.) This was said to have been the stronghold of King Curaoi Mac Daire, whose wife signalled to her lover, Cuchullin, that the menfolk were away and the place easy to storm, by pouring milk into the mountain stream (called Finglas-white water).*

21 Ballycatteen ring fort at Ballinspittle, county Cork. The smaller 'forts' have only a single bank, but the bigger have several, breached by elaborately constructed gateways. Ballycatteen has been excavated and dated to c AD600. The owners lived in huts inside the enclosure, and under the huts there was, as in so many of these places, an underground passage or souterrain. Like Garranes, also in county Cork, this 3 acre site seems to have been a craftworkers' centre for metal work rather than a homestead. The excavators thought it might also have served as a stronghold for the area in time of attack. Continental trade was indicated by fragments of wheel-made pottery thought to have come from Gaul, and a fragment of glazed, pale yellow pottery probably from a Lower Rhine factory. Occupation continued, off and on, for a considerable time, well after the central date of 600.

22 Knockashee in county Sligo. This flat topped hill has not only some Megalithic cairns on its summit but a whole series of hut circles, perhaps marking the homes of the cairn builders. This picture is a good example of how faint earthworks, hard or impossible to see on the ground, show up from the air.

3 FROM ANGLO-NORMAN CASTLE
TO BIG HOUSE

The ancient Irish did not live in towns. Town life came in with Viking invaders and raiders who settled where you might expect, at ports along the coast. The big Irish seaboard towns have Viking roots, and sometimes Viking names—Wexford and Waterford are Norse. In 1170 the Anglo-Norman invasion began, and the Anglo-Normans were also townsmen as well as castle builders. The nucleus of many old Irish towns was the little walled city; Dublin and Galway, Limerick and Waterford are examples.

The potential of such places to the seaborne Vikings is obvious, but only detailed study of vertical air photos really shows up the lines of the original little walled nuclei of the old cities. You do not see it immediately when flying over them; more obvious is the present-day suburban sprawl: the long quay sides, container ports and tower buildings.

Other Irish towns grew in other ways. Round great monastic church centres like Armagh (where the line of the whole hilltop fort wall still shows in the street patterns); or at crossroads where fairs were held, or at a garrison town. Very many Irish towns and villages are simply lines of houses along the sides of a road or a crossroad. Few have the shapely, almost English style, 'round the village green' plan of Sneem in county Kerry (plate 43).

The countryside itself is patterned with medieval ruins as well as far older ones. The Anglo-Normans first built themselves defensive 'motte and bailey' strongholds. A wooden castle stood upon an artificial mound and there was a surrounding outer defensive earthenwork. Some were placed on older fort sites and their green mounds still show up in many parts of Ireland. But very soon, the Anglo-Normans, and the Irish landowners too, built themselves castles in stone. Some of these are very large, with inner keeps and circling walls—Cahir in county Tipperary is one such, and the best preserved. Roscommon is a vast ruin with a fairly typical history: built originally in 1269 by Robert Ufford, Justiciary of Ireland, it later became the fortress of the O'Connors, rulers of Connacht, and was finally blown up by Cromwell's forces in 1652.

As well as a considerable number of such large castles, there is an inordinate number of small castles, little grey towers, ruggedly built. Like the ring forts, they had a long life—'tower house' describes them very adequately. Within, you may yet stand on the vaulted stone floors of some of the storeys, and see also where intervening wooden ones made yet other floor levels and rooms. The roof timber is still there at Dunsoghly Castle, a familiar holding point to light aircraft using Dublin airport. In fact, Dunsoghly, or Plunkett Castle, was inhabited until comparatively recently and is a very fine example of the little Irish tower house. The chapel alongside is dated 1573, some hundred years after the tower.

From the air one sees just how such castles, large and small, were strategically placed; can pick out details of obliterated walls, and see them in plan, as their builders conceived them. This is true too of the later defences around Ireland; for instance the half-buried defences guarding the entry to Cork Harbour,

23 *Athy, with the Barrow passing through the town, and the Grand Canal in the foreground just above its junction with the river. The tilted roof, like the fin of a shark, is the new Dominican church, a 'modern' design copied from a continental original and hardly suited to Irish topography. But it is perhaps no worse than the 'conventional' design of the modern Athy parish church seen further off.*

still cared for by the Irish Army. Of earlier date is the starfish design of the old James Fort at the mouth of Kinsale Harbour, and across the inlet the complex, now roofless, buildings and heavy walls of Charles Fort, the construction of which began in the 1670s.

In a more peaceful Ireland, the big landowners built themselves great houses; huge palaces like Castletown (begun 1721) in county Kildare or Carton (1739) in the same county, or the many lesser, simple yet gracious Georgian houses that still dot the Irish countryside. Often surrounded by parkland, green sward and fine trees, they add to the beauty of Ireland from the air in no small measure. Some of these big houses were burned out during the 'Trouble' years and stand as raw shells. Some are now state property and have become national Forest Parks: Rockingham on Lough Key on the Shannon headwaters; Woodstock on the river Nore. The big house at Woodstock

24 The bridge complex at Monasterevan. The Grand Canal did not immediately join the river Barrow at Monasterevan where they met, but was carried over the river, and then alongside it, only finally joining it at Athy. Here the railway bridge is seen in the foreground (the railways killed barge passenger services quickly), the canal aqueduct beyond it, and the road bridge (carrying the main Dublin-Cork, and Dublin-Limerick, road) beyond that. The Grand Canal Company's Standing Orders of 1786 resolved that 'a lamp be erected at Monasterevan where the Passengers land out of the Passenger Boats and that Mr Bean be requested to provide a Globe or Lantron with six Burners to light the Passengers to and from the Boat to the Inns at Monasterevan in the mornings and evenings'.

is a mere shell but the great arboretum, begun in 1831, is now cared for by the Forestry Division of the Department of Lands, as well as extended round about in ordinary commercial plantations. Woodstock in late autumn is a forest of brilliant colours, gold, orange and scarlet, cut through by a great avenue of silver firs and another of the green brushes of monkey puzzles, one of the few long avenues of the latter trees that exists.

Yet other big houses, built later, aped earlier styles: the mock Gothic of Lismore Castle for instance, and the same style used in the original buildings of the university colleges of Cork and Galway.

In the world of the church, the coming of the Anglo-Normans brought changes, an end of the indigenous 'Celtic Church' monasteries (which might, left alone, have continued to exist) and the coming of the continental religious orders. Before the Normans came, St Malachy was involved with a movement of reform and renewal in the native Irish church, and was responsible for introducing to Ireland the Cistercian Order (1142) and the Canons Regular of St Augustine, who may have arrived a little earlier. The Canons Regular, secular clergy living in community, not monks, took over a great many of the old Celtic Church monastic sites. A fine church of theirs stands, circled by the old

25 Cahir in county Tipperary, on the river Suir (caher, cathar—fort). Here a town grew up round first a rath, and then the great medieval castle whose original construction goes back to the twelfth-century work of Conor O'Brien, lord of Thomond. It is a typical large Anglo-Norman castle, exceptionally well preserved, on the river bank, beside the present main road (Cork-Dublin) bridge.

monastic rath wall, on Canon Island in the Fergus, close to Shannon airport; they were also on Inisfallen at Killarney.

Then the friars arrived, Dominicans in 1224, Franciscans in 1231 or 1232. The remains of their many foundations are everywhere to be seen; the massive, some-

31

26 *Waterford city. The modern city is a progressive industrial centre (among other things, the home of Waterford cut glass) and container port (see also plate 42), but it is one of Ireland's first towns, a harbour settlement made by the Vikings. Reginald's tower (bottom right, at road corner by quays) is said to have been built by Reginald the Dane in 1003. The old walled city, enclosing some 15 acres, lay along the banks of the Suir. The place was captured by the Anglo-Norman leader, Strongbow, who repaired and rebuilt the walls and Reginald's tower. Some sections of old wall can yet be traced on the ground but are hardly visible from the air.*

In English the town still bears its Viking name of Waterford, but in Irish it is Port Lairge, Large's Landing Place.

times even fortified, churches and abbeys of the Cistercians, the old Dominican churches and the more numerous Franciscan ones graced with tall, graceful towers. From the air, one can trace the foundations of priory buildings now all pulled down, or fields and walls round the old monastic centres. The typical Dominican or Franciscan church was a long, rather narrow church with a transept, and a tower set where nave and transept crossed; the conventual buildings, where the friars lived, were arranged around a rectangular cloister garth, very often on the north side of the church. Some of these old abbeys and friaries were in the cities; many more in the open countryside, where they yet stand, graceful still in ruin, set off by the green fields. One large Franciscan one, well preserved, is on Sherkin Island off the Cork coast.

The Reformation began the process, prolonged in Ireland which resisted strongly, of the decay and ruin of these old buildings; it cannot be said that the new churches and buildings of the churches and religious orders in Ireland come anywhere near the grace and style of the old ruins.

The railway enthusiast will set about

tracing the lines of the various light railways that once travelled adventurous routes in various parts of Ireland. Much more obvious, and for the most part still navigable, are the canals. Recall that when the canals were first begun there were no Ordnance Survey maps of the quality we now have; that the surveyors must have worked very much in the dark in planning their lines; and marvel when you leave Dublin and see the great canal line, straight as a ruled line, heading over the bogs and plains to join the Shannon.

The Grand Canal, begun in 1756, links Dublin with the Shannon which it reached, at Shannon Harbour, in 1804. A branch line runs into the river Barrow. Thus it became possible to come from Waterford by river and canal both to Dublin and across to the Shannon, and so north or south along that river. To make the Shannon navigable, various works were done on the river itself—deepening the old fording places, for instance, and unearthing a number of archaeological 'finds', things dropped by centuries of men crossing on foot or horseback or small boat.

The Grand Canal is now being used by sailing enthusiasts in increasing numbers. The Royal Canal from Dublin to Mullingar and Termonbarry on the Shannon, begun in 1789, took a far less potentially profitable line and is now largely abandoned. The North

27 The Woodstock Arboretum on the banks of the River Nore. Here the 'Great House' is today a mere ruin, and the forest taken over by the state. It is now one of the most interesting Forest Parks in Ireland. The collection of trees was begun in 1831 and includes, as is seen in this autumn photograph, an avenue of monkey puzzles (left) and another of silver firs (right).

28 Small tower house or castle on Galway Bay at Kinvarra. There are vast numbers of such small fortified places all over Ireland—the famous Blarney 'Castle' is one such. This is a particularly fine example, set on an islet and with a well-preserved wall around it. The picture also indicates typical county Galway fields of this district on the edge of the Burren hills (opposite).

29 Settlement pattern on the lowland of Connemara between the Twelve Bens and the sea on Galway Bay, alongside one of the complex sea inlets. The seaweed can be seen as a dark line on the rocks along the shore. Some of the bare rock is probably due to cutting of peat and 'scraw' for fuel. The fields form a kind of mosaic of stone-walled irregular enclosures, with twisting laneways or boreens between them. Superimposed on the old irregular field pattern is a newer, re-allocation and rationalisation of land in a series of straight fences re-dividing the old holdings. In the Aran islands, people still own a field here and a field there, not one continuous farm plot, and on the mainland this system also once existed in some places. Old style and modern houses can also be seen in this photograph (above).

30 'Sancta Maria de Petra Fertili', St Mary of the Fertile Rock, the Cistercian abbey of Corcomroe in county Clare, founded in 1182. This beautiful ruin is placed in a fertile valley back from Kinvarra under the bare limestone hills of the Burren. A springtime photograph with the hawthorn (may) in full flower in the hedges. (Gorse does not grow on the limestone of Burren but blackthorn and hawthorn, with their white blossom, abound.) This view suggests older field divisions under the modern rectangular pattern.

had other canals, one from the head of Carlingford Lough to bring shipping up to Newry, as it still does, another from Lough Neagh to Lough Erne. Various other canal

lengths were dug for various purposes—for instance to bring coal from the mines on Lough Allen side into the Shannon navigation.

Along their lines are the sharply humped little bridges that carry roads over the thin canal lines, the locks, and the great hotels that once served the passengers in the fast 'fly boats' that careered across Ireland, horses towing at the gallop, and made the magnificent speed of 10mph. One such canal hotel has been restored by local effort at Robertstown in county Kildare and made a centre of continued interest in Irish 'canaliana' and canal preservation and use. The canal engineers carried the Grand Canal into the Barrow in a curious way, running it parallel with the river, which it did not join until Athy, but crossed by an aqueduct at Monasterevan. That town is a complex of bridges, roads and waterways; canal, river, railway and road meeting and crossing each other.

One factor of Ireland's history is always present in some shape or form: the way the land is used, the pattern of field and village, the distribution of bog and forest and farmland. Field patterns are very interesting. In the stone-rich districts the walls are of stone, usually picked off the fields they surround, and these stone-heap walls may be immensely thick. In very mountainous land, the wall stone collections will be supplemented by cairns of more stones dumped on rock outcrops in the actual field enclosure. These walls may be very old, and from the air it can be seen that these old enclosures usually follow rather irregular patterns. More modern fields, created by re-allocation of land, the need for larger field units and more modern farm methods, are usually very regular and as such, stand out strikingly. Sometimes a new field system can be seen superimposed on an older one.

In mountain country, the way in which the farmers worked as far as they could into the

31 The 'Great House'. The De Vesci family still live here, in the house built in 1773 by the first viscount as a wedding present for his wife. The grounds, with a remarkable collection of trees and shrubs, are open to the public. Abbeyleix, in county Laois in central Ireland, was one of the first estates to go in for commercial tree growing.

32 *The ruined Cistercian abbey of Bective on the banks of the river Boyne, set in typical rich Meath pastureland. The Cistercians were the first of the continental religious orders to establish themselves in Ireland. Their Bective foundation was made in 1146. The place was partly rebuilt in the fifteenth century and altered again in the sixteenth century when it passed into lay hands. It is interesting not only as a well-preserved ruined abbey, but as a fortified abbey built to resist attack in troubled times.* hills is shown clearly by the little green fields working up the valley heads and finally ending, fairly high, against the rough brown of the moorland. Yet higher are traces of old fields and 'lazy bed' ridges, long abandoned, with memories of over-population and famine, of men desperately going that high to work any land they could and scratch from it enough potatoes for survival.

4 TOWN AND COUNTRY

Air survey has very obvious uses in the planning of roads and urban development. From the air, the whole map comes alive, and the potential of use and misuse can be taken in at a glance. It is less obvious how the aeroplane reveals pollution, whether in sea, river or air. For instance, the city of Cork, lying in a long valley, seems often to have a temperature inversion in the air above it, trapping smoke over the city, smoke which then drifts down-wind, along the valley line. Flying into Cork from the north, the city's position can often be picked up from far off by this smoke bank.

Along the coast after heavy rain, one can see the turbid, mud-laden waters of the big rivers fanning out far into the sea at their mouths; or gain a vivid impression of the scale of fish destruction in certain polluted and green algae-infested lakes.

The use of land, even the machinery working it, can be equally well studied. The different crops in the fields—young oats, barley and wheat are even of different greens —can be easily identified. In late summer the country becomes a patchwork of golden fields of grain and green pasture. Irish farming, for the most part, is highly

33 Settlement and field patterns in Glencolumbcille, county Donegal. Fields on the dry land of a low hill circle the raths and ruined church of an old monastic establishment, probably founded by the great saint of Donegal and of Iona in Scotland, Colmcille (Columba). The sea comes into a bay below; above the settlement are two natural, morainic bars, but the long white ridge of stones is due to pilgrims visiting the holy well beside it, each adding one to the pile. The pilgrimage, on St Colmcille's day, 9 June, still takes place.

34 *Glencolumbcille, county Donegal, a view up the valley to the village. Note the fields made between the outcrops of ice-rounded rocks. This place was dying rapidly, with insufficient work to make a worthwhile living, and with young people being forced to emigrate, until its energetic priest, Father McDyer, organised a co-operative and set a target for renewal in such western mountain districts. Activities range from knitwear to growing celery for canning, and recently the start of a 'Rent an Irish cottage' tourist scheme. The cottages, Irish style, with all modern conveniences, have been built on the floor of the valley in the middle of the picture (see also plate 4).*

35 *Ireland supplies herself with sugar from home-grown beet. An autumn shot of the Thurles sugar-beet processing factory in full swing at harvesting time.*

mechanised, and combine-harvesters and silage cutters move steadily over the corn and grass.

There are now extensive areas under forest, and one can see all their history, from the first draining and ploughing of mountain land, through the young trees, to the fully grown forest. Though much of this afforestation is of commercial plantations of conifers, their green expanses add much to the beauty of the country seen from the air. In the case of the Slieve Bloom mountains in the central plain, the woodlands spreading up each

valley, high toward the crests, have transformed a rather monotonous expanse of heathery upland into a series of green, tree-grown valleys from which the final ridges lift in purple or brown contrast. The new Forest Parks, developed to provide amenity as well

41

as timber, add to the beauty of the forest scene; whilst in Kerry, at Killarney, and in Wicklow, some native woodland still clings to the hillsides. At Killarney, the woodland on the hillside is of oak and arbutus, with hazel and alder, and on Muckross peninsula is an ancient forest of yew trees.

Very large areas of Ireland are covered with bog. There is bog upon hilltop and hillside as well as covering vast areas of the central plains. This has been cut by hand for fuel for centuries, and the hand-dug cuttings show up all over the country. Today the great bog areas are being worked mechanically on a large scale by Bord na Mona, the Turf (Peat) Board. Special machines have been devised to work upon the soft ground and cut the turf. This is variously processed as machine-cut turf, providing the familiar sod for the domestic fire; as milled peat to fire furnaces; as compressed peat in briquettes, now much used in the home. The peat is used to operate a number of turf-burning power stations producing electricity for the national grid.

37 Post World War II industrial development in Ireland includes, in Cork Harbour, a new dockyard and, here seen distantly, an oil refinery. The latter refines all the oil used in the Republic. Irish Steel's works are on Haulbowline island in the middle of the photograph.

38 *Cobh in Cork Harbour, the transatlantic liners'*
point of call, and town of departure for many
generations of Irish emigrants. The town is built
in terraces on the hillside. The cathedral of St
Colman was built between 1868 and 1919 in French
Gothic style; it has a notable carillon of forty-
two bells. Irish Steel's works are on Haulbowline
island opposite, an island now joined to the
mainland by a new bridge. Cobh, the name means a
haven or cove, was for a brief period, following
Queen Victoria's visit to Ireland, known as
Queenstown.

Bord na Mona's operations in the central
plains have a striking appearance. One looks
down on great expanses of brown peat from
which the surface skin of grass and heather
has been removed, and sees the brightly
coloured machines moving steadily over it,
cutting the sod. Experimental work too is
being done to develop the techniques of
turning 'cut away bog' into farm land, when
all the peat has been harvested.

Power is also obtained from the great rivers
of Ireland. The first hydro-electricity scheme
was one to harness the river Shannon at
Ardnacrusha, where the river plunges suddenly down towards the sea after meandering
with little change of level across the central
plains. The Ardnacrusha scheme was constructed between 1925 and 1929. More

43

39 Letterkenny in county Donegal. An amorphous spread of recent building from the original nucleus of a line of houses along the mainstreet—one of the longest in the country. The town is near the head of the sea inlet, Lough Swilly, on the river Swilly. Inland the small fields of Donegal stretch away toward the mountains in the west.

40 Kenmare, 'the head of sea' at the head of the sea inlet of the Kenmare 'River' in county Kerry. It shows an early example of town planring. Its origins go back to the grant of the place in 1670 to Sir William Petty who started smelting iron there. The iron ore was imported and the smelting carried out with charcoal from the surrounding woods. Charcoal-burning is an activity that is partly responsible for the modern absence of woodland in Ireland.

The town was built later to a definite plan; it is particularly attractive in spring when the double pink cherries, planted along the streets, are in flower.

41 *Building styles in an Irish town. University College, Galway in Victorian sham-Gothic, with the new tower-style hospital buildings behind it.*

42 *The ancient city of Waterford has a modern container port (right bank of river) handling a considerable amount of traffic. Reginald's tower, dating from Viking times, can be seen on the opposite bank of the river Suir.*

43 *Few Irish villages are as attractive as Sneem (An tSnaidhm, the 'knot'), with its two village greens and two churches—the large Roman Catholic one on the lower right, and the little towered Church of Ireland (Anglican) by the river bridge. A long inlet up which ships used to sail, comes up from the Kenmare 'River' to Sneem which is placed under the rise of the Kerry hills on the road from Kenmare to Waterville on the 'Ring of Kerry'.*

recently other rivers have been harnessed for power: the Liffey at Pollaphuca, the Lee at Iniscarra (both with the flooding of the valleys above to form reservoirs), and the Erne at Ballyshannon. Of the areas submerged, the Blessington reservoir above Pollaphuca is said to be clear enough at times to look down and see the old field walls below the water.

Since World War II many new industries have been started in Ireland, often with foreign capital and expertise. Irish industry now includes both the old ship-building yards at Belfast and the new, post-war one at Cobh in county Cork; the deep sea oil terminal with giant tankers serving it on Whiddy Island in Bantry Bay; and the oil refinery at Whitegate in Cork Harbour. Television masts rise from many high points to give coverage to the whole country. A network of wires carries electricity to nearly every home. Ireland now is a land of many contrasts: of the new tower buildings, the new factories, and the equally new 'Rent an Irish Cottage' groups of traditional thatched houses — with all modern conveniences attached.

Air traffic is served by four major airports, fully equipped with radar and navigational aids. Aldergrove (Belfast) on Lough Neagh in the north, Dublin, Cork and Shannon are the four, but they are augmented, for small aircraft, by a whole string of lesser fields. There are two 'baby airports' with good tarred runways at Castlebar in Mayo and Farranfore in Kerry, and also a series of grass fields which, by 1971, gave fairly complete coverage of the country for a light plane.

Roads, and the amount of traffic using them, are, of course, obvious from the air. Northern Ireland has a length of motorway, but most Irish roads are of rather even and good quality, so that it is sometimes quite difficult to distinguish main road from

44 Afforestation: Dromore (the name means the big ridge). This place was once a stronghold of the clan O'Mahoney and is now a state forest with new forest plantations fanning out from the original privately owned woodland and gardens. It is one of the Forest Parks open to the public with lay-by picnic areas and walks. There is access to the shore of the sea inlet of the Kenmare 'River'. Again, a windy day with spume streaks parallel to the wind direction.

45 *More typical of an Irish village is the cross-roads type of growth, here seen at Timoleague, county Cork, on a sea inlet on the south coast. Timoleague is Tigh Molaga, St Molaga's House, and originated as a monastery founded in the sixth century by this saint. Later, a Franciscan friary was built on the site; its graceful ruins with typical Franciscan slender tower stand by the shore. Inland, the Roman Catholic church has a modern version of a round tower for belfry.*

by-road. There are rather few old, disused 'green roads', and one sometimes feels that every road that Ireland ever constructed is still in use and maintained in good order! In the country, people tend to live well spread out, on farms or in small clusters of houses as well as in villages and towns, and this network of roads is very necessary to link all these homes.

5 IN THE TRACK OF THE ICE

Possibly the best place to begin a study of the Ice Age of the past is with the present; with the Swiss Alps where the snow packs into ice in the hollows of the mountain sides, or in Greenland where the land is submerged by a vast ice sheet, round the edge of which the mountains rise clear. In Ireland it is easy to follow the tracks left by the ice once some sort of mental picture is established of what ice, in vast masses, looks like and can do.

Not quite all of Ireland was submerged under the Ice Age ice sheets, but most of it was. Some part in the south-west stood clear, and the highest peaks, like those of Greenland, rose above the ice and took the full force of the intense frost, shattering the rocks into the splintered ridges that today are a delight to climb.

Ice acts like a vast rasp as it moves over the country. It picks up stones and grit and scours the rocks bare and smooth as it pushes over them. By sheer weight and the abrasive dirt it carries, it moulds the land,

46 The deep ravine known as the Horses Glen was cut in Mangerton mountain, Killarney, county Kerry, by a small local glacier working its way into an original hollow on the hillside. The rounded shoulder of the 2,756ft Mangerton probably preserves its pre-Ice Age shape. The photograph shows the head of the Horses Glen and across a narrow col, the ice-cut hollow of the Devil's Punch Bowl from which Killarney draws its water supply. In this winter picture the snow shows up the weathering peat hag banks of the boggy summit of Mangerton. In the distance is the Lower Lake of Killarney and the Muckross peninsula.

47 Two esker ridges in county Mayo on the central plain of Ireland. Esker, an Irish word, means a long narrow ridge or embankment of gravelly material. Their most probable origin is in under-ice rivers: streams flowing under the ice sheets and depositing material along their lines. Eskers carry Irish roads over bogland in some places. Quarrying of the more distant esker is shown in this picture— they are an obvious source of sand and gravel.

whether of soil or rock, over which it moves. This ice moulding is very obvious over large areas of Ireland when viewed from the air.

In the north, extending from the country round Belfast Lough and Mourne, across by county Cavan and down to Donegal Bay and Clew Bay, is the drumlin belt. *Drumlin* is Irish for a little ridge, one of the words (with esker) taken from Ireland into international terminology. Drumlins are little ridges; the land corrugated by the passage of the ice sheet to give this 'basket of eggs' topography; ridge upon tiny ridge, all much of the same height and sometimes with complex lake systems in their hollows. At Donegal Bay and Clew Bay the ridges run down into the sea and form islets. In all, the drumlins cover some 4,000 square miles, one-eighth of the total area of Ireland.

But where the rock lay much nearer the surface, the ice smoothed and rounded the bed rock itself. In Cork and Kerry, great areas of mountainous land show this smoothing, moulding, rounding, the forming of 'roches moutonnées' (sheep rocks, from their shape). On a clear day, over this sort of terrain, you gain an extraordinary impression of the power and extent of this glacial smoothing and moulding of the bed rock.

Where the glacier tongues ploughed through valleys, they changed the whole shape. The Gap of Dunloe is a fine example but there are many others. The ice-shed, the parent mass of ice, then lay in the Kenmare

48 The Gap of Dunloe in county Kerry. Here a shallow col through the hills was deepened and gouged out into the present rocky glen by a tongue of ice pushing its way from the 'ice shed' (the main parent mass of ice) in the Kenmare 'River', to the plains around Killarney and Killorglin. There it fanned out and came to a halt, leaving behind morainic bars where its snout stood and melted, dumping the carried material. This picture shows the Gap, with the ice-smoothed rocks, and the little lakes along the valley floor, with a suggestion higher up, of the original shallow valley. It is taken from the Black Valley, looking through to the Killarney end of the Gap.

River area and forced its way over the lower hills and through the valleys to the plains at the head of Dingle Bay. It turned the shallow valley of the Gap into a deep U-shaped one, scooping hollows along its floor in which now lie lakes, and giving it steep, precipitous flanks. From the air one can see not only the whole enormous cleft of the Gap but the line, in part, of the original shallow valley from which it was hewn.

Where the ice melted, it deposited all that was in it. The sheer dirt of a melting glacier

49 In the Wicklow mountains: the beautiful corrie lake of Lough Tay. The Wicklow mountains, a great ridge of granite, are noted for the beauty of their valleys and their corrie lakes, of which this is one.

snout has to be seen to be believed, whilst the water from it is turbid with fine silt, 'glacier milk'. Anywhere that the ice spread out, melted, and continued to do so for a length of time, all this material—sand, gravel, stones—was deposited and formed moraines. There are many such moraines on the plains at the head of Dingle Bay, around Killorglin and Killarney; green ridges of sand and gravel rising from the lower, boggier levels, with their green, dry, farmland standing out vividly. In the general melting at the end of the Ice Age, the caught-up material was deposited everywhere to form boulder clay, which covers a great deal of the country.

Another very curious feature are the long, green, railway-embankment-style ridges.

These are the eskers. Some of them carried ancient roads; some still carry roads, dry routes across the bogs. The Esker Riada, an esker line from the Dublin area to Galway Bay, provided a good route across the central part of Ireland, east to west, by dry ground, from very early times. Clonmacnois, the famous early monastery, sits upon green grassed, dry, gravelly, morainic material along this line, on the bank of the river Shannon. Eskers seem to have been formed by rivers running under the ice sheets and depositing sand and gravel along their courses.

Not all the south-west was ice covered. Here it is possible that some plant and animal life survived from pre-glacial Ireland, including the Kerry butterwort (*pinquicula*

50 Drumlins, Irish for 'little ridges', cover some 4,000 square miles of Ireland, one-eighth of the whole country. They extend across the country to Donegal and Clew Bays. They are ridges formed by the passage of the great ice sheets over the country during the Ice Age. Some are entirely composed of soil, clay and gravel; others have a core of bed rock. Here the drumlin 'swarm' is seen coming down to the sea in Donegal Bay, the final drumlins forming islands therein.

grandiflora) and the arbutus. The peaks of Ireland's highest mountains, the 3,000ft MacGillycuddy Reeks in Kerry, stood clear, *nunataks*, above the ice, and were fretted into knife edge and pinnacle by frost. The sudden change from ice-smoothed rocks to frost-riven ones is easily seen—around 2,000 to 2,500ft up the slopes.

51 *Not all of Ireland was covered by the Ice Age ice sheets. Parts of the south-west remained ice free and the higher ridges of the mountains formed nunataks above the glacier fields, as in modern Greenland. So the lower ground is intensely rounded and smoothed by the passage of the ice, whilst the higher rocks are fretted and riven by frost action. The picture shows part of the land that stood above the ice sheets—the undulating ridge of the MacGillycuddy Reeks in county Kerry. The ragged line of the ridge that stood above the ice can be clearly seen, whilst below are corrie lakes in hollows gouged out by small, local mountain glaciers. This picture was taken from over the Gap of Dunloe, looking along the ridge over Knocknapeasta. (See also plate 65 of Carrauntual.)*

These high mountains, during glacial times, nourished their own glaciers. Snow packs into the hollows of the mountains, beds down into ice and this, freezing, melting, refreezing, eats down into the bed rock. As the snow piles up and beds down more

54

and more, it begins to move slowly out from the hollow, downhill, in a glacier tongue. Much of the beauty of the Irish mountains is derived from the corries and the corrie lakes cut by ice at various times during the Ice Age.

The lakes may be contained wholly within a rock basin, or the water held back by the green bar of the moraine where the glacier melted at its snout. The pilot can look into these corries in a way no climber can, see their sheer walls, the lake, the moraine where the glacier came to a halt, and see it set off against the whole mountain chain in which

it lies. There may be a series of corrie lakes stepped one above the other, as along the hills from Mullaghanattin back of Sneem to Waterville in county Kerry. But the most magnificent series of corrie lakes is found in the Horses Glen on Mangerton mountain at Killarney. The rounded shoulder of this hill

52 When the ice began to melt at the end of the Ice Age, the melt waters cut many temporary channels which are now dry, or nearly dry 'wind gaps'. A detail of one such dry valley cut through the rocks is shown here—the Scalp at Enniskerry, just south of Dublin.

seems to retain its pre-glacial shape. A small local glacier cut into the heart of the hill, trenching out the vast curving hollow of the Horses Glen, with three lakes, at different levels, lying along its floor. Across a col at the valley head, another glacier cut out the hollow of the Devil's Punch Bowl from which Killarney draws its water supply.

The Comeragh mountains in Waterford have very fine, 'text book' corries and lakes, of which the most famous is Coumshingaun, with a cliff rising about 1,000ft behind its dark little lake.

53 The Drumlin belt ends in Clew Bay, county Mayo, where the ridges form islands, one of which is shown here in close-up. The material of which it is composed can be seen in the cliff section whilst on the island are the tents of a colony of hippies.

An enormous amount of water was locked up in the ice that once covered Ireland, and when the melt began it had to go somewhere, and often, since unmelted masses of ice remained, by very different routes from the present drainage systems. The country has many dry 'wind gaps' through which turbid water from melting ice once poured and cut these channels.

In the south of the country, unmelted ice remained in the hollows of the inlets of Bantry Bay and the Kenmare River, and the melted water had to go up the valleys rather than, as with the present drainage, down them. This melted water, escaping toward Glenflesk in the Roughty Valley at the head of the Kenmare River, cut the deep spillway of Cromagloun near Kilgarvan, and from the Bantry area, the straight rock cleft

through the ridge of the pass of Keimaneigh. Even better known temporary drainage cuts of melting ice water lie in county Wicklow, close to Dublin, in the ravine of the Scalp and the steep-sided wooded valley of the Glen of the Downs.

54 The Glen of the Downs, county Wicklow, a fine example of a spillway cut by glacial melt waters. It carries a road, and the woodland is a Forest Park area. In the distance is the quartzite peak of the Great Sugar Loaf mountain.

6 THE MOUNTAINS

The highest mountains of Ireland only just top the 3,000ft contour; the highest of all is, on the present maps, 3,414ft, but less by the more accurate measurement of the most recent survey. But their low altitudes must not deceive either pilot or climber; these little hills can and do behave with all the savagery of high mountains. In Kerry the climber can still come on the wreckage of World War II aircraft that flew into the steep hillsides when coming in across the Atlantic. Fierce winds can channel down the valleys or sweep, like surging water, over the ridges, so that the air around the hills is turbulent as a mountain stream, and up-draught or downdraught can be so powerful that a light plane's engine is unable to hold a level path through it.

The mountains that rise along the western seaboard are the first high ground met by moisture-loaded winds coming in off the sea. As the air flows over the mountains, it cools, the moisture condenses in part, and the familiar cloud caps form on Mount Brandon—at 3,127ft Ireland's second highest mountain—and the other ranges. Some Kerry people say of Brandon that there is never a day without cloud, and never one without a clearance of some sort. Yet on the right day, with clear air, clear skies and calm winds there is no danger. Geology, geography, vegetation type and distribution, all these can be studied; and withall, the breath-taking beauty of the Irish mountains.

The mountains are small but very indi-vidual, and each has its own special character, setting and history. Most of the mountain lines lie along the coast, so that the beauty of the hills is set off by the beauty of the sea, strand, cliff and offshore islet. The inland ranges are less striking, but the highest of them, the Galtees, rise in a graceful ridge of high grassy peaks with corrie lakes under their cliffs.

The Mourne mountains in the north-east are geologically the youngest of the Irish hills. There is a great complex of Tertiary igneous rock in the area, gabbro and granite, and the rocks at Slieve Gullion in Newry show the same concentric ring patterns (cone sheets and ring dykes in geological termino-logy) as those of the same period in Scotland, in Ardnamurchan and Mull. For the gabbro of Carlingford and the granite of Mourne belong to the same series of intrusions that built the Giant's Causeway and Staffa, the high ridges of the Cuillin hills in Skye, and the rocks of the Scottish Arran and St Kilda.

The Mourne mountains themselves appear as great brown, rounded ridges, broken here and there by granite tors and scarred with the pale wounds of granite quarries. Mourne 'paved Lancashire' as the saying goes, for the hills are close to the sea, and it was easy to export setts. The 'stone boats' that took out Mourne granite, brought in Welsh slates to replace the older traditional thatch of Mourne cottages.

On the highest point, Slieve Donard, 2,796ft, are the remains of two Megalithic chambered cairns, later adapted by St Donard to form a mountain-top hermitage. This was once, like Slieve League, Mount Brandon and Croagh Patrick, the objective of a mountain pilgrimage in the saint's

honour; today only the two last named pilgrimages continue, Croagh Patrick attracting many thousands of climbers each summer.

The granite of the Wicklow mountains and the Blackstairs mountains, lying between Dublin and the southern Wexford coast, is far older than that of Mourne, and the shape of the mountains very different. This granite is of Caledonian age, intruded during the great mountain building movements that came before the Carboniferous age, movements that gave to the north of Ireland its marked north-east south-west mountain trend lines. In the south, later, Armorican

55 Outside of the MacGillycuddy Reeks, the highest mountain in Ireland is Mount Brandon, 3,127ft, which thus ranks as the second highest mountain chain. It is a great ridge, running from north to south across the Dingle peninsula in county Kerry, and is frequently cloud-capped, being the first high ground met by moist air coming in off the Atlantic. On the actual summit is a spring of water, now a holy well, and the remains of an early Celtic hermitage supposedly founded by St Brendan the Voyager.

This picture shows the whole ridge from the north cliffs, looking south to Dingle Bay. It provides a wonderful ridge walk on short green turf and moss. The slopes are fairly gentle toward the west but fall in great cliffs to the east.

59

56 Snow and sunshine and clearing morning mist on the Slieve Mish mountains in the Dingle peninsula, county Kerry. The Slieve Mish rise to 2,798ft, and are noted for their sheer flank falling to Tralee Bay, from which this photograph is taken. The 'headland fort' of Caherconree lies just out of the picture to the right (see plate 20). The ridgewalk of the Slieve Mish is easy but commands great views over the Kerry Hills, Dingle Bay and north toward Aran and Connemara.

(Hercynian) mountain building movements, coming after the Carboniferous, put the very obvious east-west trend lines on the southern hills.

The Wicklow hills rise to 3,039ft in Lugnaquilla, and in Mount Leinster, in the Blackstairs, to 2,610ft. The Wicklows are great rounded heathery uplands and their interest is in their valleys which are hollowed into typical glacier-deepened U-contours, with waterfalls dropping from the cliffs on either side. The shape of the valleys and the rivers with their falls, the corrie lakes high in the hills, and St Kevin's great monastic site at Glendalough, are the main points of interest in flight over these hills. For the record, the Wicklow granite covers some 625 square miles, and is the largest outcrop of granite in Ireland and the British Isles. The granite, where it came in contact with the sedimentary rocks into which it was intruded, hardened and altered them to the point where they became more resistant to erosion than the granite itself. The result is that the rock around the rim of the hills is the harder, and has produced much of the wild scenery of the Wicklow glens, which soften in character as they penetrate into the heart of the hills. Typically, the glen of the east side of the Wicklow mountains—Glenmacnass, Glendalough, Glenmalure—is long, straight, ice-eroded into a U-shaped trench, with the tributary streams coming into it in cataracts down the steep flanks, and near its head a marked change in level of the valley floor with a waterfall in the main stream.

Along the southern coast, the mountains are very different, the sandstones and conglomerates of the Comeraghs forming a great escarpment facing eastward, with a series of beautiful corrie lakes tucked under its cliffs as well as under the lesser crags on the western side. The summit, rising to 2,597ft, is a wet heathery plateau of peat hags. Today the peat is not growing on these high places, but being eroded into typical hags—islands of heather-topped turf banks with peaty morass, or even the underlying rock and gravel between. Such erosion can be seen even on the narrow ridge of the Galtees further inland.

In Kerry, where the long ridge of the MacGillycuddy Reeks undulates at about the 3,000ft contour, and rises finally to Carrauntual's 3,414ft, the Irish hills are at their most beautiful and most dramatic.

57 Errigal, 2,466ft, in Donegal, is probably the most startlingly dramatic of all Irish hills, rising in a kind of Matterhorn upthrust of a narrow peak mantled with white quartzite screes. However, by going around to its back, one may gain the top quite easily by a gentle ascent.

58 In Donegal, the mountains of Muckish, Aghlamore, Aghlabeg and Errigal, rise dramatically and singly from the lowland, and show markedly the north-east to south-west trend imposed by the ancient Caledonian mountain building movements. This flat-topped peak is Muckish, the pigs mountain, 2,197ft.

59 Ireland's most magnificent sea cliff is certainly that of Slieve League (Flagstone mountain) in Donegal. This falls 1,972ft from summit to sea in steep crags. Like Croagh Patrick and Mount Brandon, it has a summit hermitage of the early Irish church but the rather scrappy remains do not show up well. This picture shows the whole ridge and cliff of Slieve League.

That long ridge, part a broad and grassy walk, part a narrow rocky knife-edge, seems to take on a quality almost of movement. The corries and their lakes on either flank can be seen in all their beauty and detail and the whole scene has a magical quality about it. It is an outlook that ranges from the low-land with its farms and fields to the high tops and then out to sea to the Blasket islands at the end of the Dingle peninsula, and yet further, to the rocky fangs of the Scellig rocks.

These hills of west Cork and Kerry are built of sandstones and conglomerates, with a volcanic felsite forming a cliff of cream-coloured columns in little Bennaunmore between Mangerton and Crohane. The hills spring up suddenly from the Kerry lowland and Carboniferous rock; the junction is a line of thrust and movement between Carboniferous and Old Red Sandstone that can be traced into Wales and on into France.

In good weather too, the magnificent corrie series on the lesser ridges of Kerry, from Mullaghanattin to Waterville, can be explored, as well as the mountains of the Beara peninsula, where county Cork marches with Kerry. This is a desolate upland of moor and ice-smoothed rock outcrops, with, on either side small lakes under rocky crags. Below are little fields and farms that form a narrow border to the mountains between them and the long sea inlets of Bantry Bay and the Kenmare 'River'. Hungry Hill, 2,251ft, at the peninsula's end is a great round lump of a hill with two lakes cradled in ice-smoothed rocks half way up its flanking cliffs. From them, a thin waterfall drops some 700ft to the valley below—a place of pilgrimage to Victorian Irish tourists, especially when it was in spate.

It is more difficult to get a cloud free view of Brandon, just across Dingle Bay from the

60 Ben Bulbin (1,730ft) overlooking Sligo Bay is a very different mountain from any others in Ireland. Here is a range of green limestone hills with flat tops and steep escarpment flanks. Ben Bulbin itself forms a prominent nose or snout projecting over the plain fringing the coast.

61 *A detail of the escarpment of the Ben Bulbin mountains in county Sligo. This shows both the cliffs and screes and the field pattern below.*

Reeks, but when it is clear the great ridge with its ruined summit hermitage of Celtic Church times is a magnificent sight. Across the Conor Pass is a lower line of hills with more fine corrie lakes tucked in under their crests. One can look over these hills to the more distant prospect across Dingle Bay, to Carrauntual and the Reeks, and down to the west to the Blaskets which, seen end on from the northern sea cliffs of Brandon,

appear as part of the mainland, as indeed they once were. Not until further on do the sea channels between them come into view. These Kerry hills are mostly green grassy mountains, good for sheep, but with heather in great purple spreads here and there. They are utterly different from the low hills (whose highest point is Slieve Elva, 1,133ft) of the Burren to the north in county Clare.

The Burren is a limestone karst; its bare summits of pale rock, scree edged, are fringed below with dense scrub wood. In spring most of Ireland is gilded with furze blossom; but once in the Burren there is no sign of

64

this shrub which dislikes lime; there is only the white blossom of blackthorn and hawthorn. One suspects that the Burren is a fairly recently eroded area due to tree cutting and overgrazing, for a spider's web of old fields and raths goes high to very bare rocky ground, suggesting that when this was inhabited, it was much more productive. The old fields and raths of the Burren uplands are perhaps their most interesting feature and one which can hardly be appreciated to its full extent from the ground.

Across Galway Bay are different rocks and very different mountains including the grouped quartzite summits of the Twelve Bens (2,395ft), the long ridge of the Maumturks, and beyond, the graceful arc of the highest mountain in the area, Mweelrea (2,688ft). These hills, the ranges separated by deep narrow glens, rise suddenly from the flat lowland of Connemara, a maze of moor, lake and rock with little farms and extensive turf cuttings. The Twelve Bens and Maumturks are of pre-Cambrian quartzite, hard rock that stands high above the lowland outcrops of granites and schists of the same period. The quartzite also forms the hills of Achill island and the great humpy masses of the Nephin mountains north of Clew Bay, and yet again, those dramatic peaks of Donegal, Muckish, Aghlamore and Errigal.

62 The pilgrim path climbing the final cone of quartzite screes to the summit chapel of Croagh Patrick. Originally there would have been a cluster of beehive cells and a chapel or chapels, like those still seen in ruin on Mount Brandon (plate 64), but these are now virtually obliterated by the new chapel for summit Masses, and the booths for refreshment and souvenir sellers. On the further side of the cone is Roilig Muire, where the 'round' of the pilgrimage traditionally ended, and which preserves more of the ancient structures.

In Donegal, the north-east—south-west Caledonian trend line is very evident in those last three peaks. From far off, one sees their crests standing in line, a horizon of strange shapes; the lump of Muckish, the shapely peak of Errigal. Again, the hills rise from a lowland, a peneplain at around the 200ft contour. This harsh flat land can be seen all along the western coast, in the Rosses and

around Gweebarra Bay, and it has a certain northern barrenness lacking from even bleak terrain in the south of the country. The small island of Ireland shows quite a marked difference between north and south in climate and in the kindliness of environment; a quick flight north to south is one way to realise vividly how much difference there is, for the wilds of Donegal are far harder places to live in than the wilds of Kerry.

Croagh Patrick, 2,510ft, is another quartzite peak, a graceful mountain rising from the southern shores of Clew Bay. The pilgrim path shows as a white gash up its flanks, and there is a chapel on the summit. On the last Sunday of July many thousands of pilgrims, some barefoot, climb the mountain on a great national pilgrimage in honour of St Patrick who is believed to have spent Lent on the mountain. Many climb up the night before and remain on the mountain until the first masses are celebrated in the

63 The Connemara mountains in county Galway. Here the rocks are pre-Cambrian schists, granites, the Connemara 'marble' and very hard quartzite. The latter forms the mountains of the Twelve Bens (left) rising from the lowland of the softer rocks. The whole area has been heavily glaciated, and the Twelve Bens were themselves once a centre of the ice sheets. The Bens rise to 2,395ft. To the right is Glen Inagh and beyond it, Mweelrea (2,683ft) which stands at the mouth of the fiord of Killary Harbour. In the foreground are Derryclare Lough and Glendollagh Lough (nearest camera).

64 The summit of Mount Brandon with the ruins of St Brendan's hermitage. Like Croagh Patrick, this is a place of pilgrimage, though today only a small group climbs up to pray here. The hermitage is set at the cliff edge. Within the inner enclosure are the ruins of a beehive vaulted oratory, some beehive cells, the well, and a big cairn put up by the Ordnance surveyors who rifled the ruins for it. Right, at the crag edge, are two trenches and these can be seen to form two faint outer walls circling the inner one and settlement. Thus the hermitage seems to have the same basic plan of a cliff edge settlement as Dun Aengus (plate 19) and Caher-commaun (plate 13), though on a smaller scale.

chapel. Booths with permanent drystone walls and with temporary tarpaulin roofs on the big day, sell refreshments and rosary beads and medals. The little stone pens could be puzzling if one did not know what purpose they served.

Another pilgrimage mountain, Slieve League on the north coast of Donegal Bay (1,972ft), descends in great cliffs from its summit to the sea below. On the hollow of sheltered land back from the cliff edge, are the remains of the hermitage with a holy well, once the goal of a pilgrimage which has now died out. Little of the structure shows from the air, though one can see the outlines of a couple of beehive cells. Most of the mountain is of the Donegal schists, but there is a little Carboniferous rock remaining on the summit, showing how later strata, now all eroded away, must once have covered all these heights. Here too is a trace of the 2,000ft peneplain level. There are various peneplain levels to be seen in Ireland, levels to which the land has been, at various times, worn down to a certain uniformity. One is the 200ft one of the Rosses, another the 1,000ft moors below Errigal; and in the south, yet another at 600-800ft. From

the air, these old levels, sometimes with the rivers entrenched in them, are very evident.

Slieve League's sea cliff is the finest in Ireland, and certainly one of the most magnificent in both Britain and Ireland put together. It rises sheer from the sea, narrowing along its summit to a thin knife-edge at one point, called the One Man's Path.

Between the quartzite hills of Donegal and those of Mayo in the south, are the limestone heights of Ben Bulbin in county Sligo. They are different from the bare karst country of the Burren; Ben Bulbin (1,730ft) is a flat-topped mountain ending in a sharp snout facing the sea, with steep escarpments edging its tableland. Below is Lough Gill, with Yeats' island of Inisfree, and the woods on the

65 Ireland's highest mountain, Carrauntual, 3,414ft, in snow. In the lower foreground is the ridge to Caher (3,200ft); Carrauntual itself is centre right, and the ridge extending from it to Beenkeragh (left) is 3,314ft. The ridge is a narrow knife-edge of rock that stood above the Ice Age glaciers, and is one of the more exciting traverses in Ireland.

lower hillside bright perhaps in autumn tints.

It is this extraordinary contrast, a thing basically geological, that is at the heart of the attraction of the Irish hills; the possibility of ranging, within a short distance, from the green tableland of the Ben Bulbin hills to the sea cliffs of Slieve League or the heathery hump of Nephin, lifting in circular isolation from the lowlands.

68

7 IRISH RIVERS

Irish rivers are particularly suitable for study and exploration from the air. By no other means can one achieve anything like a full and comprehensive understanding of their peculiar routes. None of the big rivers makes its way into the nearest sea. Most of them rise somewhere in the central plains and amble sluggishly over them, before making a final cut through the coastal hills to reach the sea. Thus in technical terms the upper part of the river may be 'senile', whilst the final reaches are those of a young river actively cutting its line through its gorge, broken by falls. It is these falls, of Shannon and Erne, which have been harnessed for hydro-electricity schemes.

From the air one can see the whole line of a river. Over much of Ireland, where the rivers flow in the flat inland country, it is

66 The river Slaney entering the inlet of Wexford Harbour at Ferrycarrig, county Wexford. The picture shows typical fields of this county, the 'garden' of Ireland. The castle on the right is claimed to have been the first Anglo-Norman castle erected in Ireland. On the left, the round tower commemorates Wexford men who died in the Crimean War.

67 The historic town of Trim on the river Boyne. Its origins go back to very ancient times—a ford on the river above the present town. Fortified by the Anglo-Normans, on the edge of the English Pale, it is a town whose history is involved with all the twists and turmoil of the whole story of the Pale and English involvement with Ireland. The castle covers 2 acres and is said to be the largest in the country. Across the river, the Yellow Steeple of St Mary's Abbey marks one of the several medieval religious houses of the town.

impossible otherwise to get a picture of what they are about. The air allows one to see the river as a whole, how its line is adjusted, or maladjusted to the terrain through which it flows, and to follow many other details of interest. Floods are impressive; one can survey just how far they extend and often make out the basic river line within the spread of overflow water. Again, meanders may be seen in plan as also can old meanders, where the river has swung away and left its earlier track in green hollows beside its new course.

There are very many lakes in Ireland, and these spread into several vast inland seas. These expansions along the river Shannon will be dealt with in the next chapter, but there are the others—Lough Neagh in Northern Ireland; Lough Conn between the Nephin mountains and the long, heathery upland of the Ox mountains; Loughs Mask and Corrib which set off the rise of the Connemara mountains to the west of them.

The Bann is involved with Lough Neagh. It is one of the rivers that do rise in the high hills near the coast, taking origin in the Mourne Mountains in the Deer's Meadow hollow. It flows down into the lake, and emerges on its northern shore, to reach the sea at Coleraine on the north coast of Ireland.

The Slaney too rises in the high hills, on Lugnaquilla on its Glen of Imaal side, in the Wicklow mountains. A thin line of silver water, it then flows southward, by Baltinglass,

Tullow and Bunclody, cutting a line through the Leinster granite between the Wicklow hills and the Blackstairs. Then, around Enniscorthy, it develops into a broad waterway trenched into the land and heading out into the complex inlet of Wexford Harbour.

The Liffey behaves differently. Again, it

68 The mouth of the river Boyne. Up river the smoke of a large cement factory can be seen, and beyond that, Drogheda, the first point at which the river was bridged. Identified with the Inver Colpa of ancient geographers, the Boyne was an important entry point to Ireland and a known landfall on the Irish Channel. (See also other Boyne photographs, plates 1, 32, 67.)

originates in the Wicklow hills, at their northern, Dublin, end. Its upper reaches are now damned into the Blessington reservoir, with hydro-electricity works at the Polla-phuca waterfall below. It is thought that the original pre-glacial Liffey flowed out north-wards through the Brittas col. The King's river, however, cut back into the Liffey and captured it. Then, with glacial deposits left after the Ice Age blocking the old river lines, the combined streams cut a new way out by Pollaphuca. The Liffey descends to the plains and swings on a wide arc, by Kilcullen, Newbridge and Leixlip, to run east to the sea through the heart of Dublin.

The Boyne on the other hand, rises in the bogs, the traditional source being Trinity.

72 *The Bandon river at Inishannon in county
Cork. Here the river which has been flowing from
west to east, swings sharply south to the sea at
Kinsale. Irish rivers seem to have originated on a
now totally eroded surface of younger rocks and so
have been superimposed on the older surface
below, to which they have had to adjust. Shipping
used to come up this long entry into county Cork
and there are numerous old wharves along the
river from Inishannon down to Kinsale.*

Well, a holy well at Carbury Hill, 4 miles
from Edenderry. It makes its way to Trim
and then on an easterly course to the sea
below Drogheda, becoming more and more
beautiful as it goes. From Trim onwards, it
is a splendid river, set in a green and wooded
glen, with great houses and parkland on its
banks, as well as the Megalithic cairns at
Newgrange and Knowth.

The Three Sisters—Barrow, Nore, Suir—
all rise in the hills of the Irish heartland.
There is a kind of touch and go relationship
between Barrow and Liffey, for the Tan-
kandsgarden bog drains on the one hand to
the middle sector of the Liffey and on the
other to the Barrow headwaters. It is a very
low ridge, and if the Liffey were to rise
another 15ft it would send its headwaters
into the Barrow instead of to Dublin Bay!
These low ridges separating one drainage
system from another can only be seen fully

from the air, or drawn out in detail on the contoured map.

The Three Sisters rise fairly close together. The Suir rises on the northern end of the ridge of the Devil's Bit mountain, near Templemore in Tipperary, at about 1,200ft. The Nore rises on the south side of the ridge of the Slieve Bloom mountains, drawing in tributaries from the valleys under the summit; the actual Nore, out of the various streams that go to join it, turns south to the Devil's Bit where it ends about a mile from the Suir's source. The Barrow originates on the north side of the Slieve Blooms, and again its headwaters are less than a mile from the heads of Nore tributaries.

Each river makes its own line to the sea but the three join forces again in Waterford Harbour. In their lower reaches they are wide waterways and were, in the not so distant past as well as in prehistoric times, used as such. There are odd lengths of old canalisation along some of the rivers to

73 Holycross Abbey on the river Suir in county Tipperary. This was a Cistercian house, named from its possession of an (alleged) relic of the True Cross. Remains of frescoes have survived on its church walls. In 1970 work was started to re-roof and restore the building to church use. This photograph was taken in late 1970 at the beginning of the work.

74 *Clonmel—Cluain Meala, 'Honey Meadow'—on the river Suir. Shipping used to come this far up-river and it was also the first base of Charles Bianconi's system of horse-drawn 'cars' which, in pre-railway days, eventually extended all over Ireland. When the railways did come, the 'bians' formed connecting links with the new transport service. Here too, the writer George Borrow passed some of his boyhood, and Laurence Sterne was born (in 1713).*

75 *Carlow on the river Barrow. (For other Barrow pictures see plates 6, 23, 24, 79). The town, on an important crossing of the river, has the ruin of a large Anglo-Norman castle, dating from the thirteenth century and standing out boldly in this picture with its twin drum towers.*

76 *Fermoy on the river Blackwater, the greatest river in county Cork. During the days of British rule, Fermoy was an important garrison town.*

help shipping, on the Boyne for instance; and one can spot the old wharves where the small coasting ships tied up. Higher up there were once many mills worked by water-power, and their ruins often stand out boldly.

The peculiarities of the Three Sisters can best be seen by taking Waterford as the starting point, and flying up the Suir, with the ridge of the Comeraghs on the one hand and the rounded hump of Slievenamon on the other, tracking the river by Carrick-on-Suir and Clonmel, till it swings north for Cahir, and on, past the great citadel of the Rock of Cashel with its chapel, cathedral and round towers, and so by Thurles to the Devil's Bit mountain and the source. The trickle of the Nore can be followed east and then south; by the beautiful woods and house

77 Lismore Castle on the Blackwater. The castle (mostly a fairly modern reconstruction) is owned by the Duke of Devonshire. This is a good example of how air photography can show the plan of a large building and its gardens.

of Abbeyleix; by the historic city of Kilkenny, and by the arboretum of Woodstock where the river begins to trench itself into the 200ft peneplain upland level. It emerges into the Barrow just above New Ross, and one looks down a wide glittering seaway to the open ocean beyond Waterford. Here one can turn up the Barrow, its meanders entrenched into the land, past the old Celtic Church site of St Mullins, past Graiguenamanagh and Carlow and Athy to Monasterevan and the river's swing west to the Slieve Blooms. The Barrow, linked by the Grand Canal to Dublin and the Shannon Navigation, was until very recently carrying commercial barge traffic—it still carries pleasure sailors. In its lower reaches, again with woodland and hillside to set off the river, it is very beautiful, and some of the last of the 'Barrow boys', the old barge crews, boasted that it could give Killarney best. Yet another twist to the study of the strange paths of Irish rivers can be achieved by heading away east from Athy to pick up the Slaney coming down from Lugnaquilla, and by trailing this down to the sea at Wexford, on a parallel course to the Barrow, and coming back to the south coast a short distance away from where this up and down flying of the Three Sisters began.

Irish river development is partly conditioned by the present shape of the country and its modifications by glacial deposits. But the river systems seem to have originated on younger rocks which are now entirely eroded away, so that a system of drainage which developed on them, was then let down and superimposed on the rocks below. This is very obvious in the southern rivers of Bandon, Lee and Blackwater.

78 A small dam and reservoir on the river Liffey at Leixlip. This is a Norse name meaning 'salmon leap'—lax, a salmon. The modern Irish name means the same thing but is translated into Irish, Leim an Bhradain. The modernised castle is on an ancient site and incorporates some of the older structures—it goes back to one first built in the twelfth century by Adam FitzHereford, a follower of Strongbow.

The original mainline streams seem to have flowed from north to south, with others coming into them from east and west. But now these east-west lines carry the main rivers—along the very marked hollows of the ridge and hollow pattern of the south in county Cork. These ridges and hollows are geological folds, anticlines (arches) and synclines (the hollows between the ridges), whose axes run east-west—the trends established by the Hercynian folding mentioned earlier. They provide an obvious compass direction and guideline, and along their hollows flow the Bandon, the Lee and, greatest of the Cork rivers, the Blackwater. Near their mouths these rivers revert, with a sudden right-angle bend, to the old north-south line and plunge suddenly for the south

79 *The lower Barrow runs with entrenched meanders, in a course cut deep in the general level of the countryside. Here at St Mullins are the remains of a famous early Irish monastery, and alongside it at the left, a motte.*

St Moling, or Mullin, was one of the most famous of seventh-century Irish saints, and died in 692 or 697. The monks ran a free ferry service across the river, and like so many Irish saints, Moling is hero of many animal stories—a pack of foxes once receiving monastic hospitality. The old wall of the monastic enclosure can still be partly traced—the line of thick trees to the right of the church. Beside the latter are the remains of other old churches and the round stump of a round tower. A pilgrimage in the saint's honour still takes place on the saint's day, 17 June, and on 25 July when St Moling is said to have blessed his completed mill and millstream.

coast. The Lee makes the turn at the head of the complex inlet of Cork Harbour; the other two much further inland. The lower part of the Blackwater is trenched deeply into the general 200ft level of the surrounding countryside. The east Cork river Bride comes in along this lower section of the Blackwater line, and sweeps, in wide curves, up an open valley to Tallow. In the old days, when coastwise shipping carried what now goes by road, little ships used not only to make their way up the wide Blackwater, but up the Bride too as far as Tallow.

The river Erne originates, heading north-west, in a complex of drumlins and lakes in county Cavan, a complex that enlarges into Upper Lough Erne. It then narrows again, widens to the more open waters of Lower

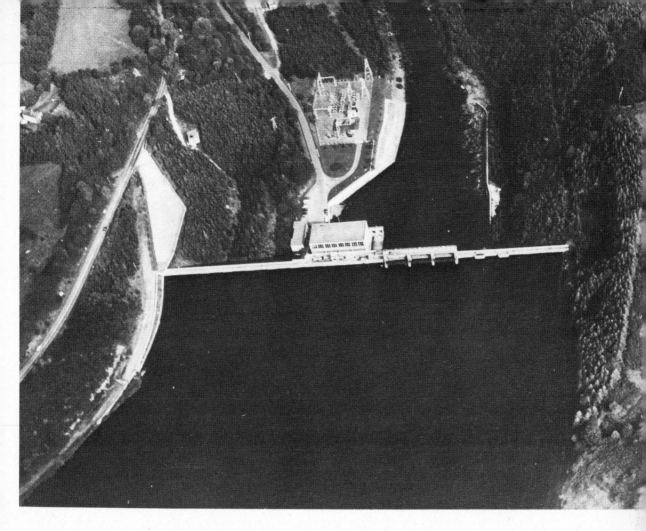

Lough Erne, and then enters Donegal Bay by the brief length of true river, now harnessed by the hydro-electricity scheme at Ballyshannon. The drumlin/lake complex or maze of Upper Lough Erne is well indicated by the fact that the islands cover 5.3 square miles in a lake area of 29 square miles, whilst

80 The Iniscarra dam and power station on the river Lee in county Cork. This makes a considerable contribution to the Irish national grid.

the shore line is 100 miles long. In times of flood, a rise of 10ft in the water level doubles Upper Lough Erne's total area.

8 THE LORDLY SHANNON

The Shannon is the largest river in Great Britain and Ireland. It flows from north to south for the best part of 200 miles down the very centre of Ireland, a roadway and a barrier; a river of Irish history. It ambles over the central plains, falling only 55ft in 100 miles but, where it breaks through the hills at Killaloe, dropping 100ft in 20 miles—it is here that the Ardnacrusha power station is sited. It was always a river one could sail up; a watery highway through Ireland, along whose banks are a whole litany of early monasteries. Boatloads of foreign pilgrims came to Clonmacnois according to the old Irish records of the Celtic Church. Where there were shallows and a ford—the greatest is Athlone, originally Ath Mor (the Great Ford)—early sailors, including the Vikings, could carry a light boat around them. Later the Shannon Navigation deepened these shallows to allow barge traffic to get through, or made parallel lengths of canal.

The river was a roadway into the Irish

81 Lug na Sionna, the Shannon 'Pot'. This pool under the Cuilcach mountains is the traditional source of the river Shannon.

heartland, but it was also a barrier between east and west, with only a few places easy to ford or possibly to bridge where dry esker ridges ran either side of the broad stream. So the crossings, the fords, the bridges, were important and often heavily defended against the wild Irishry of the west, by inhabitants of the east based on the English Pale.

The Shannon is one of the great flying experiences of Ireland. South from Carrick-on-Shannon on a clear day, one looks over the vast, seemingly endless central plain of Ireland which fades into blue distance and here and there rises into sudden groups of hills. Across this vast level is thrown the silver Shannon, its gleaming water pushing

82 The Shannon flows from the 'Pot' to Lough Allen. Just above that lake, the river is seen winding between low hills on which is a network of ancient fields and 'forts' (old fortified ring homesteads). Here also runs the Black Pig's Dyke, an old Ulster boundary line.

southward, broadening into flashing mirrors of lakes and narrowing again, rimmed by the great bogs with Bord na Mona's cuttings, and by the green eskers at Clonmacnois, or the quiet meadows of the Goldsmith country east of Lough Ree.

To name a source for any great river is really rather an arbitrary exercise for they grow from a multitude of streamlets and

83 *Inchcleraun on Lough Ree, river Shannon. This is a typical old Celtic monastic ruin, with an enclosing round outer wall and a group of old churches inside it. Traces of old dividing banks within the enclosure can also be plainly seen. It is possible that there has been some change in water level since the place was built—otherwise it suggests a three-quarter circle backing on to the shore rather than a complete round enclosure.*

84 *Shannon Bridge on the river Shannon below Clonmacnois. Here the esker ridge crosses the river and provides a dry foothold on either bank for an important bridge. Note the old fortifications on the western bank. The river itself is running in spate, high-lighting the lift of the drier ridges.*

85 *Lanesborough on the Shannon above Lough Ree. This town has experienced economic renewal owing to its being in the heart of extensive Bord na Mona turf cuttings. Note the large power station connected with these activities.*

springs, but the traditional source of the Shannon is worthy of that great river. One discovers it, after a little searching, under the brown uplands of the Cuilcagh mountains, and among many lakelets and streams —a round pool from which a sizable stream flows forth down the valley and is named Shannon. This round pool is Lug na Sionna, the Shannon Pot.

The Black Pig's Dyke, an ancient defensive earthwork of the Ulstermen, crosses the country where this infant Shannon enters the first lake of its course, Lough Allen. The dyke itself is not easy to spot, but the little ridges of hills here are all covered with ancient walls and raths which stand out boldly in winter or spring when vegetation is at its shortest.

Lough Allen lies amongst the hills, with the workings of the Arigna coalmines on

86 *Iniscealtra on Lough Derg, the greatest of the 'inland seas' on the Shannon's course. This, like Clonmacnois, was another very important early monastic site. There are remains of a round tower and early churches, which are enclosed in their own boundary walls. The whole island is crossed by the lines of old field banks probably related to the monastery. Excavation began here in 1970— hence the white central area to be seen in this picture.*

one side. Beyond, there is Carrick-on-Shannon and the river winding over the endless plain, broadening into Lough Boderg and Lough Bofin (the lakes of the red and white cows respectively), and finally enlarging into the island-studded inland sea of Lough Ree above Athlone.

At Carrick, another river comes in to join Shannon. The main stream is augmented by

the water from Lough Key, together with that of the river that flows into it at Boyle, from the crannog (lake dwelling)-studded Lough Gara higher up. Lough Key has on its shores the Rockingham Estate, now a national Forest Park, with fine grounds and beautiful woodlands. Lough Key is very lovely indeed, with trees and wooded islets, and so too is Lough Arrow just the other side of a low ridge at its head. The low ridge between Lough Key and Lough Arrow is a main watershed: Lough Arrow drains to Sligo Bay!

On the line south, there are many extensive remains of early monasteries; on Inchcleraun in Lough Ree is the old enclosing rath of one establishment; Clonmacnois, founded by St Ciaran in 545, with its two round towers; Clonfert of which only the Church of Ireland building remains, incorporating a wonderful Romanesque door, which was a great foundation of St Brendan the Voyager. On Lough Derg, Holy Island or Iniscealtra, with a round tower, are churches, each set within its own wall and the island surface showing spider-web patterns of old fields. There are numbers of others; later history stands out starkly in the massive fortifications at the bridges crossing the Shannon at Banagher and Shannon Bridge. The Grand Canal comes in, straight as an arrow, at Shannon Harbour, with the Brosna river ambling in natural curves alongside it. Power stations stand beside the bogs. Boats cruise up and down, and the new marinas show up at many of the riverside towns.

There are the two great lakes, Lough Ree, and in the south Lough Derg, the red lake. The latter is a hollow scoured out by the ice sheets and is 22 miles long, ranging from 10 to 2 miles across. Both it and Lough Ree are liable to dangerous squalls and rough 'seas', and even barges have been lost. The holiday sailor should beware of the 'open sea' areas of the river Shannon until he gains experience; the river has plenty of other, safe, water to begin on.

87 Undoubtedly the most famous of the ancient monastic foundations along Shannon was Clonmacnois founded by St Ciaran (the Younger) in 545. It became one of the most famous of Irish monasteries, to which it is said that boatloads of foreign pilgrims and students sailed up the river from abroad. Sited on dry esker land near the river bank is a group of old churches and two round towers, though other structures such as earthworks have been obliterated by later burials. In the distance can be seen the great turf cuttings of Bord na Mona on the boglands from which the esker ridges rise. There is also a castle beside Clonmacnois. This particular day followed a night of very heavy rain, so the Shannon was in flood and the castle moat filled with water.

The hills ring the foot of Lough Derg, and the Shannon cuts through them past the little town of Killaloe, a bridge point, with the grey cathedral and oratory of St Flannan and Brian Boru's 'fort' just a bit upstream. Below can be seen Ardnacrusha power station, new canal lines to carry barges, and Limerick at the head of the tide and the long inlet of the Shannon Estuary. That estuary is over 50 miles in length from Limerick to the open Atlantic.

This whole river and estuary seems to

88 The old town of Killaloe where the river Shannon finally breaks through the coastal hills from Lough Derg and plunges steeply down for the sea at Limerick. (See also Scattery Island for a picture in the Shannon estuary, plate 18.)

provide a cross-section of Ireland, from the hills on the border with Northern Ireland, across the central plains, finishing on the Atlantic coastline between the Cliffs of Moher and the mountains of Kerry.

9 THE COASTS OF IRELAND

Even if one has made a habit of the fascinating pastime of walking along the cliffs, the first flight over them is a revelation. On a fine day, the fretting and moulding of the rocks of the actual cliff stands out in hard relief so that the whole shape is fully revealed. Moreover, it is seen in all the fulness of its beauty and colour, with a brilliant blue sea breaking white at its foot.

Of course much more shows than that. You can easily come close to what is normally inaccessible; see in a single glance things only to be got at piecemeal on the ground. Puffing holes are a case in point. Here the sea cuts a cave in under the cliff, part of whose roof falls in, providing an inland vent up which wild seas surge and fount like cold geysers.

Erosion and deposition may also be studied. Sand bars and mud flats can be seen as a whole with, in calm weather, some underwater penetration. When the tide is out, the mud is revealed with the rills

89 The curious sea lake, Lough Ine or Hyne in west county Cork. The lake is linked to the sea by a narrow and shallow channel. Its calm salt waters are ideal for marine biological studies which are carried out here. Typical ice-smoothed outcrops of rock form the rough countryside of west Cork.

90 Sea cliffs have an intrinsic beauty, emphasised in this view of the stacks and cliffs of Slieve Tooey, county Donegal. (Compare plates 3, 59 of the sea cliffs of nearby Slieve League.)

running through it in feathery lines, and one can, to a large extent, see how the deposit is being laid down and shaped. Equally, where the sea is cutting into the land, cliff falls and cliffs about to fall, the raw edges where a road or an old fort is cut across by the encroaching ocean, are all very obvious. The view of lesser islets and stacks can be surprising. Thus the Stags Rocks off Toe Head in county Cork appear from Toe Head to be substantial rocky islets, though in fact they are but the bones of islets, mere fangs of rock which only appear of any size when seen end on from the land.

In Ireland the sea is eroding the coastline at many exposed points, but at the heads of the long sea inlets, deposition of mud and sand is going on. In Kerry there are the twin sand bars of Inch and Rossbeigh reaching out across Dingle Bay, and higher, the river meandering down to the sea between wide and growing spreads of mud and meadow.

Although the Vikings gave the name fiord (now Anglicised 'ford') to several of the sea inlets of Ireland, there is only one true fiord in the country. This is Killary Harbour in Connemara, a long, narrow, winding inlet among the high hills, which threads into Leenane and whose hollow continues as a deep valley on toward Westport. A fiord is a sea inlet moulded and deepened by ice thrusting down it, so that the deepest water lies at the head where the ice pressure is greatest, and there may be quite a shallow bar at the seaward mouth.

In the south, there is a wonderful series of long sea inlets which look fiord-like, but are actually 'rias', drowned valleys. They are Dingle Bay, the Kenmare 'River' Bantry Bay, Dunmanus Bay and Roaring Water Bay. On either side the mountains rise, and further out there are islands that once must have been crests of hills that formed part of the main land. As already remarked, the Blaskets, seen end on from off the north cliffs of Mount Brandon, were very obviously once joined to the mainland.

91 A puffing hole in the cliffs of Inishturk, one of the islands off the coast of Connemara. On the spur to the right, the hole is clearly seen. It is formed by the falling in of the roof of a cave or tunnel cut under the rock by the sea. In rough weather, water would spout, geyser fashion, from the hole as the sea surges into the cave below.

92 In Cork and Kerry in the south, rocks come down to the shore but form yet another kind of coastline. This is the famous 'beauty spot' of Glengarriff (the Rough Glen) in county Cork near the Kerry border. The island is Garinish, a garden with sub-tropical plants, which now belongs to the State.

93 Pre-glacial raised beach near Courtmacsherry in county Cork. Hereabouts, the pre-Ice Age coastline followed closely the line of the present one, but sea level was a bit higher so the old beach appears as a platform just above high tide mark along the coasts of county Cork. That it is pre-glacial is shown by Ice Age deposits resting on it.

94 The sheer Cliffs of Moher in county Clare which are up to 600ft high and composed of rocks of Carboniferous age, mostly sandstones.

Roaring Water Bay itself is full of islands so numerous that they are called Carbery's Hundred Isles.

Moving eastward in county Cork from Roaring Water Bay, a rocky shelf just above high tide mark can be seen on certain sections of coast, notably between Court-macsherry and the Old Head. This is the pre-glacial raised beach. It is the wave-cut platform of the beach before the Ice Age, whose deposits lie on top of it. Here at least the Irish coastline was at much the same place and much the same level in pre-glacial times as it is now.

Thus one can explore the great sea inlets from Loughs Swilly and Foyle in the north down to the 'rias' of Cork and Kerry in the south. The Irish coast too has a great number of out-jutting headlands, the majority of

which are headland forts, whose ruins, banks and ditches across the narrowest part of the approach, show up boldly.

Again, one can study the present harbours and the shipping using them, as well as the old harbours and old ports. In Wexford, there is a series of sand-bar-locked lakes just back from the coast, and in county Cork, the curious sea lake, Lough Hyne or Ine, linked

95 In southern Ireland, the long inlets are not fiords but rias, drowned valleys. This is Dingle Bay in Kerry. Note the sandy spits coming out from Inch and Glenbeigh, and the river accumulating silt at the inlet head. There is a fine (actually stone built) ring fort on the shore at the extreme bottom left of the photograph.

to the sea by the narrowest of channels.

On the north side of Wexford Harbour are the Wexford slobs, which not so long ago were true marsh where no tractor could operate. A large part is now reclaimed farm land; two areas form a wildlife sanctuary, owned jointly by the Department of Lands and the Irish Wildbird Conservancy. One can go on foot to watch the birds. Some 6-8,000 Greenland white-fronted geese winter there, out of the world population of 15,000 of this species. To the east of the slobland is an interesting area of sand dunes, which have been partly planted with forest.

To travel along the Irish coasts is not only to see the cliffs, the beaches, the ports and the rivers winding inland, but also to en-

counter the long and varied series of offshore islets. Small islands or rocky stacks, rising from the bright sea, often complete the coastal picture of crag and strand and harbour town.

96 Yet another coastline type, where a rocky, ice-smoothed peneplain level comes down to the sea in Donegal at Dawros Head. Similar country makes up the Rosses of Donegal a little further north.

10 THE ISLANDS OF IRELAND

The island of Ireland is circled by a ring of islets, some big, some small, some mere rocks. Some are still inhabited, and nearly all of them were inhabited at one time. The landing places are often difficult of access and the seas wild; the islands themselves are fascinating, beautiful and encrusted with ancient remains of Celtic monastery or old fort. To get to some of them by sea is an adventure, and often quite difficult to organise. Although you cannot, except on the Aran islands, make a landing, and touch and walk the rocks and fields, the prowling light plane provides the easiest, cheapest, and often the most informative approach to Irish islets.

There are lighthouses on a number of the islands, and today a helicopter is used as well as a supply ship in servicing them. There is a helicopter pad and a sixth-century monastic ruin on the Great Scellig!

Irish islands are concentrated on the west and south-west seaboards rather than along the straight eastern coast, except for the complex of islets within Strangford Lough. Most northerly is the Rock of Inishtrahull off the north coast; most southerly the Fastnet Rock, with a tall lighthouse on it. The Blasket islands off the Dingle peninsula are often described as 'the next parish to America' and are the most famous in the tradition of Gaelic living and speaking.

The first thing to remember about the islands off Ireland is that in the old days they were much more attractive to settlers than they appear today. Much of mainland Ireland was heavily wooded or undrained bog. With light tools, the light soil of the islands was easy to work; it is very fertile and the access did not seem so bad to people used to getting around in small boats. The seaways were the main highways then, and the inland roads of today were hardly developed. It was not only hermits looking for rocks in the ocean who would go to an island; it was a man wanting a good farm, or a monk founding a great monastery to which people would come from far and wide. Good land, plentiful fish—the islands once must have presented a high standard of living as against that of many mainlanders, whereas today the reverse holds true. People on islands depend today on importing so many things from the mainland, and this is costly and sometimes difficult. Exporting cattle and sheep for market costs that bit extra for freight, and is troublesome. School, at least from secondary level on, means the mainland. Illness can mean a real emergency to get to a hospital. So the little islands are being abandoned and nobody now lives on the Great Blasket, to which the people first went to escape mainland rack renting and make a richer and freer life for themselves.

Off the Hill of Howth, midway down the east coast of Ireland, is Ireland's Eye (Norse, *eyja*, island), and then no more islands till one comes to Wexford and the two Saltees off its southern coast. The Saltees are low, flat islands ringed with rocky cliffs, now uninhabited. As large islands just off the south coast of Ireland they are important setting down points for great numbers of migrating birds, and so are of great importance to the ornithologist.

It is as one heads west to the coast of

county Cork that islands really begin to multiply and form a kind of fringe to the mainland cliffs and strands. Cobh, the transatlantic port from which so many Irish emigrants left for America, is itself on an island in Cork Harbour—even if it is one that is linked to the mainland by a bridge.

Further west there are the little rocks of Adam and Eve's islands in the long inlet of Glandore Harbour; High and Low Island, the latter rapidly being eroded; and then the full splendour of Carbery's Hundred Isles in the inlet of Roaring Water Bay. The latter range from islands linked to the mainland road system by bridges at the head of

97 Trawkeera Point in the Aran islands, county Galway, is typical limestone 'karst' country of bare rock pavement and stone walls. The Plassy, *wrecked off the coast and thrown by the waves high above normal tide marks, gives some indication of wave force in these parts. From* Plassy *one can trace the great boulders of the Aran storm beach along the shore line. For other Aran pictures, see plates 10, 15, 19.*

the bay, to the Fastnet rock. Between are green, fertile Sherkin beside the sailing centre of Baltimore, and high, bare Cape Clear. Sherkin was once a centre for boatbuilding—the little coasting schooners that carried trade before the coming of good roads inland—and boat building still goes on in Baltimore. Cape Clear, Irish speaking and often lashed by wild seas, is struggling to survive as an island community, and in 1971 electricity was brought to the island. The medieval church ruin by the harbour is on an older site, one founded by Ciaran of Cape Clear, 'first born of the saints of Ireland'. This Ciaran, not to be confused with the later Ciaran of Clonmacnois, sailed to the continent where he learned about Christianity, and then came back to preach it over the south, one of the pre-Patrician missionaries.

Across the bay, Long Island is a long, narrow bar of an islet off Schull. The head of the next peninsula, the Mizen, ends in a ragged horseshoe rock of an island on which the lighthouse stands, linked to the mainland by a suspension bridge.

Carbery's Hundred Isles have very marked personalities, but others here are more in the nature of chunks of mainland cut off by narrow arms of the sea. Bere Island is like that, with the fortifications of the defence works when this was an important naval harbour and base. So too is Valentia in Kerry, now linked by a bridge to the main-

98 Valentia island, county Kerry. This island is much more in the nature of a slice of mainland cut off by a narrow channel. Access to the mainland is now by a bridge. The big quarry in the foreground is the entry to the old slate mine from which huge slabs were once extracted and used, among other things, to floor London cellars and make billiard tables. Far out to sea can be seen the outline of the Scellig rocks.

land at Port Magee. The big slate quarry hole on Valentia stands out obviously from the air; it once supplied slate of high quality and in very big slabs, which was used to floor London cellars and to make billiard table tops. At the head of Bantry Bay, the green and once purely agricultural Whiddy is now an oil terminal for giant tankers.

Dursey Island off the end of the Beara peninsula, is another island struggling to survive as a community. To reach it, across the narrow sound through which the tide races, a boat must travel at an angle to the current; cattle for market were swum across behind boats. In 1969 the sound was spanned by a cable car, the first in Ireland, capable of

99 Looking along Dursey island from its further tip. The sound can just be seen separating it from the mainland. It is a high, cliffy island, with the farmland in the shelter of the ridge. The old tower on top of the ridge began a series which could pass signals on to Cork—one of the defences put up after the 1796 invasion scare.

carrying six people or one cow. Its construction offered a hope of survival to Dursey people, and the possibility of developing tourism; the population had dropped from 237 in 1861, to 53 by 1966. The island has a dramatic appearance with its great cliffs; the farm land lies in the sheltered hollow of the eastern side of the ridge, on whose top

99

100 'The next parish to America'. The Blasket islands, off the tip of the Dingle peninsula in county Kerry, are one of the most famous groups of Irish islands, though now no longer inhabited. The Great Blasket, the last to be abandoned, is nearest the mainland; further out are the smaller islands of Inishtooskert, Inishvickillane, Inishnabro and the lighthouse rock of the Tearaght. Tearaght is an island very much in the Scellig style. Note the rock arch in the middle of the island, which is thus nearly cut into two.

stands an old signal tower, first in the series of a chain that could pass a message on to Cork. It was erected against the fear of invasion at the time of the 1798 Rising—French toops landed on Dursey in 1796.

Further out to sea are three rocks called, according to their respective sizes, the Calf, the Cow and the Bull. The Bull has a great cave through its heart—the very island is an arch—and a lighthouse on top of it. It has the same craggy outline as Scellig Mhiceal, Scellig of St Michael, Little Scellig and Tearaght, all further west.

Inshore, off Derrynane is the high island of Scarriff and the lower one of Deenish, which look so hard to reach that one is not surprised that Scarriff should have a ruined Celtic oratory, but is surprised to see the very modern looking houses on it. In fact, these islands were only fairly recently abandoned by their inhabitants.

Scellig is the most dramatic of all the Irish islands, and about 8 miles off the Kerry coast. The Great Scellig is under the patronage of St Michael the Archangel, patron of high places, and it forms part of the series of mountain top shrines of Michael that run from Monte Gargano in Italy by way of Mont St Michael in Normandy and St Michael's Mount in Cornwall, to Ireland.

Five hundred feet up this sheer fang of rock are the ruins of a sixth-century hermitage, built all in dry stone, with beehive cells, two oratories, all intact to this day. Till fairly recently, people sailed out on pilgrimage to this island, and ended the 'round' of the places of prayer with a climb to the 700ft summit and the kissing of a cross cut on an outjutting rock there.

Close to the Great Scellig is the Little Scellig, whitened with the droppings of the gannets which live there. Little Scellig is the second largest gannetry in the world, with some 18,000 to 20,000 pairs nesting.

Very different from Scellig, the wild rocky hermitage set in the sea, is the monastery on Church Island between Valentia and the mainland. This is a small islet, and the wall,

monastic huts and church take up all the available space.

There are more monastic ruins of Celtic Church date on the outer Blasket islands, on Inishtooskert and Inishvickillane. Tearaght is another Scellig but Inishvickillane is green and fertile; it is said it grew tobacco but potatoes tended to run to too much leaf. Both it and Inishtooskert were abandoned in the mid-nineteenth century, and the ruins

101 Close in over the old settlement of Inishtooskert. The fields are ridged by hand-dug lazy beds. Ruins include a beehive oratory and some other buildings originally perhaps monastic and later adapted to form a farmhouse, and the old field walls. The dark growth is heather encroaching on the old fields. See also plates 109, 110.

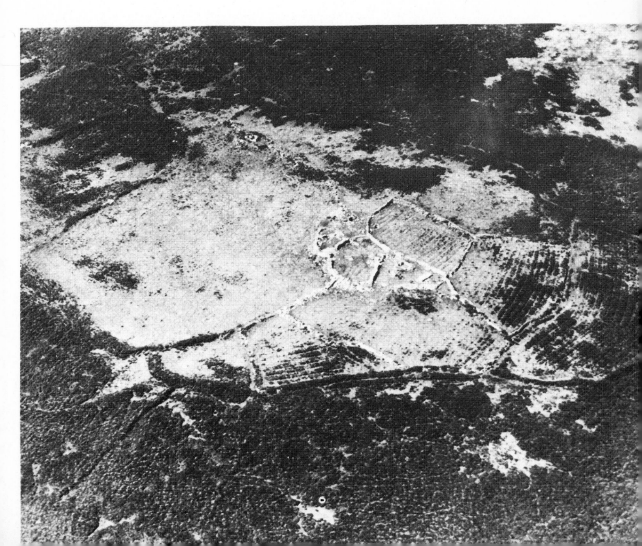

102 The Great Blasket was only abandoned in the 1950s, and its wonderful Irish community life came to an end. Its ruins are still raw and new, one of the most melancholy sights in all Ireland.

and the old fields have had time to mellow. Not so the Great Blasket, a long, green, high, steep-sided ridge of an island. Here the people had developed a remarkable Gaelic speaking community, and islanders told of their life in books: *The Islandman* by Thomas Crohane (1929), *Twenty Years Agrowing* by Maurice O'Sullivan (1933), *Peig* by Peig Sayers (1936). The English scholar, Robin Flower, wrote of them and became virtually an adopted Blasketman. *The Western Island* (1944) was one of his books. But the difficulty of island living in the mid-twentieth century became too much for the

Blasket people. The crossing, a narrow sound with a fierce current, is difficult; there was neither priest nor doctor nor nurse on the island itself. It became harder to make a living; young people left to find work on the mainland. By the 1950s, the community was running down and the last members re-settled on mainland holdings. It was a tragic ending to so remarkable and likable a community of island people. To see the island now is to feel the shock of that evacuation, for the ruined, roofless, houses of the old village are raw wounds. They have not had time to age to the grace of the old homes on Inishvickillane; they are as bitter as a town wrecked by bombing.

Another interesting group of islands are the Magharees, also called the Seven Hogs. They are a group of flat topped islands off

102

the end of the Magharee peninsula on the north side of the Dingle peninsula, a long level of dunes and fields with great sweeping white curves of beach on either side. Illauntannig, the island of St Senach, is the closest in and easiest to reach, with a not long abandoned farm, and the remains of a fine Celtic monastery built in drystone after the style of Scellig and other such sites. It stands out boldly and one can study its details and see how the sea has eaten into that corner of the island since the place was built. Illauninimill, more difficult to reach and land on, has various faint structures on it including pens for catching sheep pastured there. Gurrig, still further out, is a rugged and isolated rock of an islet.

The Irish islands are, in fact, a litany of saints' names and old monasteries. Moving north from the Magharees up the west coast, there is the great monastic island of Scattery in the mouth of the Shannon, founded by St Senan in the sixth century; and off Kilkee is the Bishop's Rock. This has the remains of an oratory on it and is obviously a stack that once formed the nose of a headland from which erosion has fairly recently isolated it. Across the mouth of Galway Bay lie the three Aran islands with Killeany, where St Enda founded one of the great pioneer monasteries of Ireland to which many other early saints came to study, and

103 Another view of the abandoned village on Great Blasket. The houses were thatched. Several islanders wrote about life on the island, as also did the well known English scholar, Robin Flower, who became more or less an adopted islander.

104 Old fields, houses, church ruin, on Inish-vickillane in the outer Blasket group. Inishvickil-lane is a green and fertile island, abandoned for over 100 years now, but once productive of milk, butter and even, it is said, tobacco. The Great Blasket islanders, after it was no longer inhabited permanently, often went there rabbiting and fishing.

105 The island of Inishmurray off the coast of Sligo. Here is the most perfectly preserved of all the large stone-built monastic cashels in Ireland. Within a massive stone fort, perhaps originally that of the local chief who may have given it to the church, is a series of churches, beehive houses and old crosses. The interior is sub-divided into sections. The islanders have now left Inishmurray for mainland holdings.

The photograph shows some older field divisions and walls running under the more modern and regular field fences.

106 The larger and more southerly of the two Saltee islands off the Wexford coast. It is an important bird sanctuary and resting place for migrant flocks.

107 Dursey Island in west Cork, off the tip of the Beara peninsula. It is separated from the mainland by a narrow sound through which the tide races making crossing difficult. This is the first island to get a cable car link, indeed the first cable car ever in Ireland. The wires can just be seen, from the two road-end houses on either side of the sound.

*108 The high cliffs of Clare Island, county Mayo.
Clare Island, in the mouth of Clew Bay, was once
the island stronghold of the sea queen, Grace
O'Malley, contemporary of Elizabeth I. The island
is still inhabited and contemplating the construction
of an airstrip.*

from which they went out to make their own
monastic foundations all over the country.
Enda may have died around AD 520.

The Aran islands are extremely interesting.
They are built of the same limestone as the
Burren and, like it, form a bare limestone
'karst' country with an exciting flora of
lime-loving and alpine plants. Aran men even
still 'make' land on the bare rock, piling on
seaweed, sand and soil; and the whole
country is a network of stone walls which
not only divide the land but are collections
of stones from it. Enormous stone 'forts'
stand out, including the half circles of Dun
Aengus.

The great cliffs of Inishmore have a
sheer fall of 200ft; on the lower cliffs is the
great storm beach of boulders cast up by the
biggest storms, well above normal tides.

The Irish-speaking Aran people inhabit
the most Irish corner of the country left, and
have a better chance of making good their
island life than the people of other islands.

They still use the curragh, the canoe made of a canvas skin on a wooden frame, descendant of the ancient skin-covered ship. When not in use they are kept on stone supports, upside down out of the water.

Killeany, on Inishmore, was the first Irish island to get a proper licensed airfield. Planes had landed on the Saltees earlier, and indeed, once or twice on Aran, but Killeany broke new ground in 1970 with its grass strip and regular scheduled air service. The Middle Island, Inishmaan, most isolated of the three and that on which J. M. Synge the playwright, used to stay, followed with its even better airstrip in 1973.

North of the Aran islands lie the islands of Connemara, built not of limestone but of the variety of ancient rocks of the adjacent mainland, and forming a complex of offshore islets, islands further out, and long involved sea inlets. Inishshark, Inishboffin, Inishturk, the big islands well out to sea, are quite incredibly bleak with their bogs and peat cuttings, and the sea snarling at the base of the rugged cliffs. It is hard to imagine people living there, yet they do, and have indeed begun some tourist business.

Clare Island in the mouth of Clew Bay, and Achill, a land of peaks and near enough to be linked to the mainland by a bridge, are much larger and more hospitable. Clare Island was the fortress home of the sea queen or sea pirate, Grainne Ni Mhaille (Grace

109 Inishtooskert was abandoned in the mid-nineteenth century; on it are the remains of an old farm, and of a far earlier Celtic hermitage site. A general view of the island. See also plate 101.

110 *Close in over Inishtooskert cliffs and this fine rocky spire. It is linked to the main cliff by an arch.*

O'Malley). Grainne once visited Elizabeth I of England, who offered to make her a countess; she refused, claiming to be herself a queen already. Grainne's exploits on sea and land are part of the folklore and history of the west.

North of the high hills of Achill, the land falls to level plains, the low peninsula of the Mullet and a string of small islets off it; all

again with the remains of early monasteries on them. Iniskea is also the wintering ground of Ireland's biggest barnacle goose flock. In county Sligo, in Donegal Bay, is Inishmurray, another island fairly recently abandoned by its inhabitants, which preserves a remarkable stone fort or cashel enclosing a group of old churches and beehive cells. Here too is an interesting series of early crosses inscribed on stone pillars, both within the cashel and set about the island. It has been suggested that this great stone fort was originally the home of the local lord, who donated it to the church. It is the most impressive example in Ireland of a big stone-walled monastery of this type. The triple-walled Nendrum on an islet in Strangford Lough is, of course, impressive too but lacks the extensive remains of Inishmurray. Muredach, the saint of Inish-murray, was possibly a convert of St Patrick or may have lived much later; virtually nothing is known of him.

In the days of the Celtic monastery, Inish-murray was a lot more fertile than it later became; for the people stripped off all the sod they could for fuel. The same process has whitened to stone level the lands of Tory off the Donegal coast. Tory looks nearer than it is: it is a good 9 miles out from the main-land, with high cliffs on the one hand, and a round tower near its landing place. It is still inhabited but is often cut off by storms. There are more islands off the Donegal coast, closer in, including another Aran Island, a big humpy island dotted with white houses. To avoid confusion with the Galway islands,

the latter are often, especially by older writers, called the South Isles of Aran.

Along the north coast of Ireland is the northerly Inishtrahull, and the much larger Rathlin island. Rathlin has a stormy history of raiding, by Norsemen, by Scots and by the English. At this point, Ireland and Rathlin come closest to Scotland, to the Mull of Kintyre, and to the Hebridean island of Islay. Rathlin is nearly Hebridean and involved with Scottish history.

All of these Irish islands have their own characteristics, beauty and interest. For the detail indeed one must land, but flight allows a complete view of the whole of them, and sometimes discovery of things hidden at ground level. Island-going by air is as fascinating and as addictive as island-going by boat.

111 The Scellig rocks are 8 miles off the Kerry coast. The little Scellig, with its rocks whitened by bird droppings, is the world's second largest gannetry. (See also plate 13.)

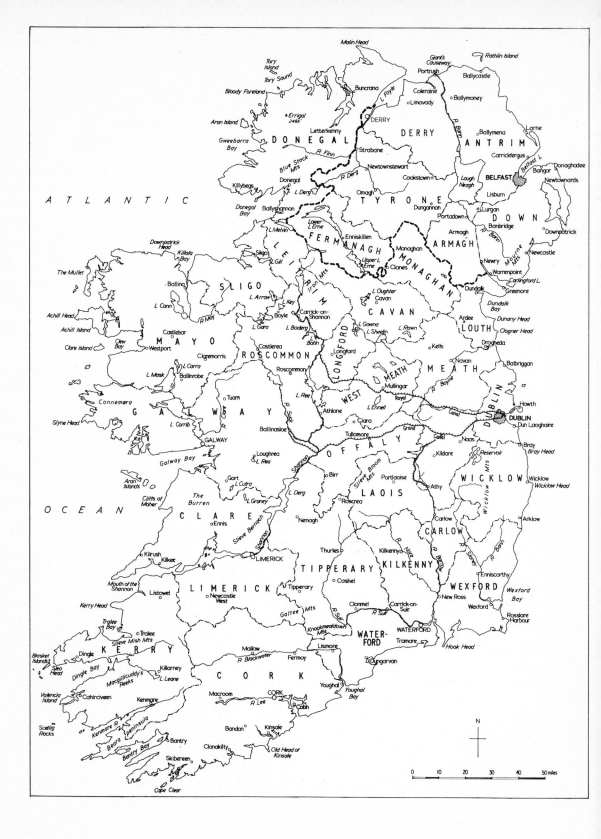

INDEX

D6